2003 SUPPLEMENT

CASES, COMMENT, QUESTIONS

CRIMINAL PROCESS

SIXTH EDITION

by

LLOYD L. WEINREB
Dane Professor of Law, Harvard University

FOUNDATION PRESS
NEW YORK, NEW YORK
2003

THOMSON
WEST

395 Hudson Street
New York, NY 10014
Phone Toll Free 1–877–888–1330
Fax (212) 367–6799
fdpress.com
Printed in the United States of America

ISBN 1–58778–625–7

TEXT IS PRINTED ON 10% POST CONSUMER RECYCLED PAPER

TABLE OF CONTENTS

*

TABLE OF CASES

Principal cases are in bold type. Non-principal cases are in roman type. References are to Pages.

2003 SUPPLEMENT

CASES, COMMENT, QUESTIONS

CRIMINAL PROCESS

*

PART ONE

INVESTIGATION

CHAPTER 1

ARREST

Page 4

Rule 3. See Appendix.

Rule 4. Rule 4(c)(2) has been amended. The amendment recognizes the provision of the Military Extraterritorial Jurisdiction Act, 114 Stat. 2488, that arrest warrants may be executed outside the United States.

For the text of the rule as amended, including stylistic changes, see Appendix.

Page 13

In Stewart v. Abraham, 275 F.3d 220 (3d Cir.2001), the court held (2–1) that the Fourth Amendment does not bar the immediate rearrest of a person on probable cause following the dismissal of a complaint against him charging the same offense and his release from custody, at a preliminary examination. The court noted that the information on which that complaint is based might be different from that presented at the preliminary examination and that the standard of probable cause was evidently different under state law from the standard for upholding a complaint at a preliminary examination.

Page 40

In United States v. Arvizu, 534 U.S. 266 (2002), the Court revisited *Ornelas* as it applies to reasonable suspicion. It said that a court should not reduce the "totality of the circumstances" test to a formula and indicated considerable deference to the trained judgment of the officer who makes a stop.

Page 41

23. United States v. Castro, 166 F.3d 728 (5th Cir.1999) (en banc).

Cf. United States v. Huguenin, 154 F.3d 547 (6th Cir.1998) (pretextual vehicle checkpoint), noted in supplement to page 155, below.

23. *Whren* is extended to a full custodial arrest, rather than a traffic stop, in Arkansas v. Sullivan, 532 U.S. 769 (2001) (per curiam).

Page 42

Atwater v. City of Lago Vista

532 U.S. 318, 121 S.Ct. 1536, 149 L.Ed.2d 549 (2001).

■ JUSTICE SOUTER delivered the opinion of the Court.

The question is whether the Fourth Amendment forbids a warrantless arrest for a minor criminal offense, such as a misdemeanor seatbelt violation punishable only by a fine. We hold that it does not.

I

A

In Texas, if a car is equipped with safety belts, a front-seat passenger must wear one ... and the driver must secure any small child riding in front .... Violation of either provision is "a misdemeanor punishable by a fine not less than $25 or more than $50." [Tex. Tran. Code Ann.] § 545.413(d). Texas law expressly authorizes "[a]ny peace officer [to] arrest without warrant a person found committing a violation" of these seatbelt laws, § 543.001, although it permits police to issue citations in lieu of arrest....

In March 1997, Petitioner Gail Atwater was driving her pickup truck in Lago Vista, Texas, with her 3-year-old son and 5-year-old daughter in the front seat. None of them was wearing a seatbelt. Respondent Bart Turek, a Lago Vista police officer at the time, observed the seatbelt violations and pulled Atwater over. According to Atwater's complaint (the allegations of which we assume to be true for present purposes), Turek approached the truck and "yell[ed]" something to the effect of "[w]e've met before" and "[y]ou're going to jail." App. 20. He then called for backup and asked to see Atwater's driver's license and insurance documentation, which state law required her to carry.... When Atwater told Turek that she did not have the papers because her purse had been stolen the day before, Turek said that he had "heard that story two-hundred times." App. 21.

Atwater asked to take her "frightened, upset, and crying" children to a friend's house nearby, but Turek told her, "[y]ou're not going anywhere." Ibid. As it turned out, Atwater's friend learned what was going on and soon arrived to take charge of the children. Turek then handcuffed Atwater, placed her in his squad car, and drove her to the local police station, where booking officers had her remove her shoes, jewelry, and eyeglasses, and empty her pockets. Officers took Atwater's "mug shot" and placed her, alone, in a jail cell for about one hour, after which she was taken before a magistrate and released on $310 bond.

Atwater was charged with driving without her seatbelt fastened, failing to secure her children in seatbelts, driving without a license, and failing to provide proof of insurance. She ultimately pleaded no contest to the misdemeanor seatbelt offenses and paid a $50 fine; the other charges were dismissed.

B

Atwater and her husband, petitioner Michael Haas, filed suit in a Texas state court under 42 U.S.C. § 1983 against Turek and respondents City of Lago Vista and Chief of Police Frank Miller. So far as concerns us, petitioners (whom we will simply call Atwater) alleged that respondents (for simplicity, the City) had violated Atwater's Fourth Amendment "right to be free from unreasonable seizure," App. 23, and sought compensatory and punitive damages.

The City removed the suit to the United States District Court for the Western District of Texas. Given Atwater's admission that she had "violated the law" and the absence of any allegation "that she was harmed or detained in any way inconsistent with the law," the District Court ruled the Fourth Amendment claim "meritless" and granted the City's summary judgment motion....

Sitting en banc, the Court of Appeals vacated the panel's decision and affirmed the District Court's summary judgment for the City....

Three judges issued dissenting opinions. ...

We granted certiorari to consider whether the Fourth Amendment, either by incorporating common-law restrictions on misdemeanor arrests or otherwise, limits police officers' authority to arrest without warrant for minor criminal offenses.... We now affirm.

II

The Fourth Amendment safeguards "[t]he right of the people to be secure in their persons, houses, papers, and effects, against unreasonable searches and seizures." In reading the Amendment, we are guided by "the traditional protections against unreasonable searches and seizures afforded by the common law at the time of the framing," Wilson v. Arkansas, 514 U.S. 927 (1995), since "[a]n examination of the common-law understanding of an officer's authority to arrest sheds light on the obviously relevant, if not entirely dispositive, consideration of what the Framers of the Amendment might have thought to be reasonable," Payton v. New York, 445 U.S. 573, 591 (1980) (footnote omitted). Thus, the first step here is to assess Atwater's claim that peace officers' authority to make warrantless arrests for misdemeanors was restricted at common law (whether "common law" is understood strictly as law judicially derived or, instead, as the whole body of law extant at the time of the framing). Atwater's specific contention is that "founding-era common-law rules" forbade peace officers to make warrantless misdemeanor arrests except in cases of "breach of the peace," a category she claims was then understood narrowly as covering only those nonfelony offenses "involving or tending toward violence." Brief for Petitioners 13. Although her historical argument is by no means insubstantial, it ultimately fails.

A

We begin with the state of pre-founding English common law and find that, even after making some allowance for variations in the common-law usage of the term "breach of the peace," the "founding-era common-law rules" were not nearly as clear as Atwater claims; on the contrary, the common-law commentators (as well as the sparsely reported cases) reached divergent conclusions with respect to officers' warrantless misdemeanor arrest power. Moreover, in the years leading up to American independence, Parliament repeatedly extended express warrantless arrest authority to cover misdemeanor-level offenses not amounting to or involving any violent breach of the peace.

. . .

... We simply cannot conclude that the Fourth Amendment, as originally understood, forbade peace officers to arrest without a warrant for misdemeanors not amounting to or involving breach of the peace.

2

Nor does Atwater's argument from tradition pick up any steam from the historical record as it has unfolded since the framing, there being no indication that her claimed rule has ever become "woven ... into the fabric" of American law. *Wilson* [v. Arkansas, 514 U.S. 927 (1995)], at 933.... The story, on the contrary, is of two centuries of uninterrupted (and largely unchallenged) state and federal practice permitting warrantless arrests for misdemeanors not amounting to or involving breach of the peace.

. . .

Small wonder, then, that today statutes in all 50 States and the District of Columbia permit warrantless misdemeanor arrests by at least some (if not all) peace officers without requiring any breach of the peace, as do a host of congressional enactments. The American Law Institute has long endorsed the validity of such legislation ... and the consensus, as stated in the current literature, is that statutes "remov[ing] the breach of the peace limitation and thereby permit[ting] arrest without warrant for *any* misdemeanor committed in the arresting officer's presence" have " 'never been successfully challenged and stan[d] as the law of the land.' " 3 W. LaFave, Search and Seizure § 5.1(b), pp. 13–14, and n. 76 (1996) (quoting Higbee v. San Diego, 911 F.2d 377, 379 (C.A.9 1990)) (emphasis in original; footnote omitted)....

III

While it is true here that history, if not unequivocal, has expressed a decided, majority view that the police need not obtain an arrest warrant merely because a misdemeanor stopped short of violence or a threat of it, Atwater does not wager all on history. Instead, she asks us to mint a new rule of constitutional law on the understanding that when historical practice fails to speak conclusively to a claim grounded on the Fourth Amendment, courts are left to strike a current balance between individual and societal interests by subjecting particular contemporary circumstances to traditional standards of reasonableness.... Atwater accordingly argues for a modern arrest rule, one not necessarily requiring violent breach of the peace, but nonetheless forbidding custodial arrest, even upon probable cause, when conviction could not ultimately carry any jail time and when the government shows no compelling need for immediate detention.

If we were to derive a rule exclusively to address the uncontested facts of this case, Atwater might well prevail. She was a known and established resident of Lago Vista with no place to hide and no incentive to flee, and common sense says she would almost certainly have buckled up as a condition of driving off with a citation. In her case, the physical incidents of arrest were merely gratuitous humiliations imposed by a police officer who was (at best) exercising extremely poor judgment. Atwater's claim to live free of pointless indignity and confinement clearly outweighs anything the City can raise against it specific to her case.

But we have traditionally recognized that a responsible Fourth Amendment balance is not well served by standards requiring sensitive, case-by-case determinations of government need, lest every discretionary judgment in the field be converted into an occasion for constitutional review.... Often enough, the Fourth Amendment has to be applied on the spur (and in the heat) of the moment, and the object in implementing its command of reasonableness is to draw standards sufficiently clear and simple to be applied with a fair prospect of surviving judicial second-guessing months and years after an arrest or search is made. Courts attempting to strike a reasonable Fourth Amendment balance thus credit the government's side with an essential interest in readily administrable rules....

At first glance, Atwater's argument may seem to respect the values of clarity and simplicity, so far as she claims that the Fourth Amendment generally forbids warrantless arrests for minor crimes not accompanied by violence or some demonstrable threat of it (whether "minor crime" be defined as a fine-only traffic offense, a fine-only offense more generally, or a misdemeanor). But the claim is not ultimately so simple, nor could it be, for complications arise the moment we begin to think about the possible applications of the several criteria Atwater proposes for drawing a line between minor crimes with limited arrest authority and others not so restricted.

One line, she suggests, might be between "jailable" and "fine-only" offenses, between those for which conviction could result in commitment and those for which it could not. The trouble with this distinction, of course, is that an officer on the street might not be able to tell. It is not merely that we cannot expect every police officer to know the details of frequently complex penalty schemes . . . but that penalties for ostensibly identical conduct can vary on account of facts difficult (if not impossible) to know at the scene of an arrest. Is this the first offense or is the suspect a repeat offender? Is the weight of the marijuana a gram above or a gram below the fine-only line? Where conduct could implicate more than one criminal prohibition, which one will the district attorney ultimately decide to charge? And so on.

But Atwater's refinements would not end there. She represents that if the line were drawn at nonjailable traffic offenses, her proposed limitation should be qualified by a proviso authorizing warrantless arrests where "necessary for enforcement of the traffic laws or when [an] offense would otherwise continue and pose a danger to others on the road." Brief for Petitioners 46. (Were the line drawn at misdemeanors generally, a comparable qualification would presumably apply.) The proviso only compounds the difficulties. Would, for instance, either exception apply to speeding? At oral argument, Atwater's counsel said that "it would not be reasonable to arrest a driver for speeding unless the speeding rose to the level of reckless driving." Tr. of Oral Arg. 16. But is it not fair to expect that the chronic speeder will speed again despite a citation in his pocket, and should that not qualify as showing that the "offense would . . . continue" under Atwater's rule? And why, as a constitutional matter, should we assume that only reckless driving will "pose a danger to others on the road" while speeding will not?

There is no need for more examples to show that Atwater's general rule and limiting proviso promise very little in the way of administrability. It is no answer that the police routinely make judgments on grounds like risk of immediate repetition; they surely do and should. But there is a world of difference between making that judgment in choosing between the discretionary leniency of a summons in place of a clearly lawful arrest, and making the same judgment when the question is the lawfulness of the warrantless arrest itself. It is the difference between no basis for legal action challenging the discretionary judgment, on the one hand, and the prospect of evidentiary exclusion or (as here) personal § 1983 liability for the misapplication of a constitutional standard, on the other. Atwater's rule therefore would not only place police in an almost impossible spot but would guarantee increased litigation over many of the arrests that would occur. For all these reasons, Atwater's various distinctions between permissible and impermissible arrests for minor crimes strike us as "very unsatisfactory line[s]" to require police officers to draw on a moment's notice. Carroll v. United States, 267 U.S. [132 (1925)], at 157.

One may ask, of course, why these difficulties may not be answered by a simple tie breaker for the police to follow in the field: if in doubt, do not arrest. The first answer is that in practice the tie breaker would boil down to something akin to a least-restrictive-alternative limitation, which is itself one of those "ifs, ands, and buts" rules . . . generally thought inappropriate in working out Fourth Amendment protection. . . . Beyond that, whatever help the tie breaker might give would come at the price of a systematic disincentive to arrest in situations where even Atwater concedes that arresting would serve an important societal interest. An officer not quite sure that the drugs weighed enough to warrant jail time or not quite certain about a suspect's risk of flight would not arrest, even though it could perfectly well turn out that, in fact, the offense called for incarceration and the defendant was long gone on the day of trial. Multiplied many times over, the costs to society of such underenforcement could easily outweigh the costs to defendants of being needlessly arrested and booked, as Atwater herself acknowledges.

Just how easily the costs could outweigh the benefits may be shown by asking, as one Member of this Court did at oral argument, "how bad the problem is out there." Tr. of Oral Arg. 20. The very fact that the law has never jelled the way Atwater would have it leads one to wonder whether warrantless misdemeanor arrests need constitutional attention, and there is cause to think the answer is no. So far as such arrests might be thought to pose a threat to the probable-cause requirement, anyone arrested for a crime without formal process, whether for felony or misdemeanor, is entitled to a magistrate's review of probable cause within 48 hours . . . and there is no reason to think the procedure in this case atypical in giving the suspect a prompt opportunity to request release. . . . Many jurisdictions, moreover, have chosen to impose more restrictive safeguards through statutes limiting warrantless arrests for minor offenses. . . . It is of course easier to devise a minor-offense limitation by statute than to derive one through the Constitution, simply because the statute can let the arrest power turn on any sort of practical consideration without having to subsume it under a broader principle. It is, in fact, only natural that States should resort to this sort of legislative regulation, for, as Atwater's own amici emphasize, it is in the interest of the police to limit petty-offense arrests, which carry costs that are simply too great to incur without good reason. . . . Finally, and significantly, under current doctrine the preference for categorical treatment of Fourth Amendment claims gives way to individualized review when a defendant makes a colorable argument that an arrest, with or without a warrant, was "conducted in an extraordinary manner, unusually harmful to [his] privacy or even physical interests." Whren v. United States, 517 U.S. [806 (1996)], at 818. . . .

The upshot of all these influences, combined with the good sense (and, failing that, the political accountability) of most local lawmakers and law-enforcement officials, is a dearth of horribles demanding redress. Indeed, when Atwater's counsel was asked at oral argument for any indications of comparably foolish, warrantless misdemeanor arrests, he could offer only one. We are sure that there are others, but just as surely the country is not confronting anything like an epidemic of unnecessary minor-offense arrests. That fact caps the reasons for rejecting Atwater's request for the development of a new and distinct body of constitutional law.

Accordingly, we confirm today what our prior cases have intimated: the standard of probable cause "applie[s] to all arrests, without the need to 'balance' the interests and circumstances involved in particular situations." Dunaway v. New York, 442 U.S. 200, 208 (1979). If an officer has probable cause to believe that an individual has committed even a very minor criminal offense in his presence, he may, without violating the Fourth Amendment, arrest the offender.

IV

Atwater's arrest satisfied constitutional requirements. There is no dispute that Officer Turek had probable cause to believe that Atwater had committed a crime in his presence. She admits that neither she nor her children were wearing seat belts, as required by Tex. Tran. Code Ann. § 545.413 (1999). Turek was accordingly authorized (not required, but authorized) to make a custodial arrest without balancing costs and benefits or determining whether or not Atwater's arrest was in some sense necessary.

Nor was the arrest made in an "extraordinary manner, unusually harmful to [her] privacy or . . . physical interests." Whren v. United States, 517 U.S., at 818. As our citations in *Whren* make clear, the question whether a search or seizure is "extraordinary" turns, above all else, on the manner in which the search or seizure is executed. . . . Atwater's arrest was surely "humiliating," as she says in her brief, but it was no more "harmful to . . . privacy or . . . physical interests" than the normal custodial arrest. She was handcuffed, placed in a squad car, and taken to the local police station, where officers asked her to remove her shoes, jewelry, and glasses, and to empty her pockets. They then took her photograph and placed her in a cell, alone, for about an hour, after which she was taken before a magistrate, and released on $310 bond. The arrest and booking were inconvenient and embarrassing to Atwater, but not so extraordinary as to violate the Fourth Amendment.

. . . [*]

Page 49

Payton. Valdez v. McPheters, 172 F.3d 1220 (10th Cir.1999) (requirement of belief that plaintiff resides at premises and is present there necessary to authorize entry with arrest warrant).

Kirk v. Louisiana, 536 U.S. 635 (2002) (per curiam) (police officers entered house to arrest defendant without warrant and seized evidence found on his person; *Payton* applied).

Page 60

Illinois v. Wardlow

528 U.S. 119, 120 S.Ct. 673, 145 L.Ed.2d 570 (2000).

■ CHIEF JUSTICE REHNQUIST delivered the opinion of the Court.

Respondent Wardlow fled upon seeing police officers patrolling an area known for heavy narcotics trafficking. Two of the officers caught up with him, stopped him and conducted a protective pat-down search for weapons. Discovering a .38–caliber handgun, the officers arrested Wardlow. We hold that the officers' stop did not violate the Fourth Amendment to the United States Constitution.

On September 9, 1995, Officers Nolan and Harvey were working as uniformed officers in the special operations section of the Chicago Police Department. The officers were driving the last car of a four car caravan converging on an area known for heavy narcotics trafficking in order to investigate drug transactions. The officers were traveling together because they expected to find a crowd of people in the area, including lookouts and customers.

As the caravan passed 4035 West Van Buren, Officer Nolan observed respondent Wardlow standing next to the building holding an opaque bag. Respondent looked in the direction of the officers and fled. Nolan and Harvey turned their car southbound, watched him as he ran through the gangway and an alley, and eventually cornered him on the street. Nolan

[*] Justice O'Connor wrote a dissenting opinion, which Justice Stevens, Justice Ginsburg, and Justice Breyer joined.

then exited his car and stopped respondent. He immediately conducted a protective pat-down search for weapons because in his experience it was common for there to be weapons in the near vicinity of narcotics transactions. During the frisk, Officer Nolan squeezed the bag respondent was carrying and felt a heavy, hard object similar to the shape of a gun. The officer then opened the bag and discovered a .38–caliber handgun with five live rounds of ammunition. The officers arrested Wardlow.

The Illinois trial court denied respondent's motion to suppress, finding the gun was recovered during a lawful stop and frisk.... Following a stipulated bench trial, Wardlow was convicted of unlawful use of a weapon by a felon. The Illinois Appellate Court reversed Wardlow's conviction, concluding that the gun should have been suppressed because Officer Nolan did not have reasonable suspicion sufficient to justify an investigative stop pursuant to Terry v. Ohio, 392 U.S. 1 (1968)....

The Illinois Supreme Court agreed. 183 Ill.2d 306, 701 N.E.2d 484 (1998). While rejecting the Appellate Court's conclusion that Wardlow was not in a high crime area, the Illinois Supreme Court determined that sudden flight in such an area does not create a reasonable suspicion justifying a *Terry* stop.... Relying on Florida v. Royer, 460 U.S. 491 (1983), the court explained that although police have the right to approach individuals and ask questions, the individual has no obligation to respond. The person may decline to answer and simply go on his or her way, and the refusal to respond, alone, does not provide a legitimate basis for an investigative stop.... The court then determined that flight may simply be an exercise of this right to "go on one's way," and, thus, could not constitute reasonable suspicion justifying a *Terry* stop. [183 Ill.2d], at 312....

The Illinois Supreme Court also rejected the argument that flight combined with the fact that it occurred in a high crime area supported a finding of reasonable suspicion because the "high crime area" factor was not sufficient standing alone to justify a *Terry* stop. Finding no independently suspicious circumstances to support an investigatory detention, the court held that the stop and subsequent arrest violated the Fourth Amendment. We granted certiorari ... and now reverse.

This case, involving a brief encounter between a citizen and a police officer on a public street, is governed by the analysis we first applied in *Terry*. In *Terry*, we held that an officer may, consistent with the Fourth Amendment, conduct a brief, investigatory stop when the officer has a reasonable, articulable suspicion that criminal activity is afoot.... While "reasonable suspicion" is a less demanding standard than probable cause and requires a showing considerably less than preponderance of the evidence, the Fourth Amendment requires at least a minimal level of objective justification for making the stop.... The officer must be able to articulate more than an "inchoate and unparticularized suspicion or 'hunch' " of criminal activity. *Terry*, supra at 27.[2]

Nolan and Harvey were among eight officers in a four car caravan that was converging on an area known for heavy narcotics trafficking, and the officers anticipated encountering a large number of people in the area, including drug customers and individuals serving as lookouts.... It was in this context that Officer Nolan decided to investigate Wardlow after observing him flee. An individual's presence in an area of expected criminal activity, standing alone, is not enough to support a reasonable, particularized suspicion that the person is committing a crime. Brown v. Texas, 443 U.S. 47 (1979). But officers are not required to ignore the relevant characteristics of a location in determining whether the circumstances are sufficiently suspicious to warrant further investigation. Accordingly, we have previously noted the fact that the stop occurred in a "high crime area" among the relevant contextual considerations in a *Terry* analysis. Adams v. Williams, 407 U.S. 143, 144 and 147–148 (1972).

In this case, moreover, it was not merely respondent's presence in an area of heavy narcotics trafficking that aroused the officers' suspicion but his unprovoked flight upon noticing the police. Our cases have also recognized that nervous, evasive behavior is a pertinent factor in determining reasonable suspicion.... Headlong flight—wherever it occurs—is the consummate act of evasion: it is not necessarily indicative of wrongdoing, but it is certainly suggestive of such. In reviewing the propriety of an officer's conduct, courts do not have available empirical studies dealing with inferences drawn from suspicious behavior, and we cannot reasonably demand scientific certainty from judges or law enforcement officers where none exists. Thus, the determination of reasonable suspicion must be based on commonsense judgments and inferences about human behavior.... We conclude Officer Nolan was justified in suspecting that Wardlow was involved in criminal activity, and, therefore, in investigating further.

Such a holding is entirely consistent with our decision in Florida v. Royer, 460 U.S. 491 (1983), where we held that when an officer, without reasonable suspicion or probable cause, approaches an individual, the individual has a right to ignore the police and go about his business.... And any "refusal to cooperate, without more, does not furnish the minimal level of objective justification needed for a detention or seizure." Florida v. Bostick, 501 U.S. 429, 437 (1991). But unprovoked flight is simply not a mere refusal to cooperate. Flight, by its very nature, is not "going about one's business"; in fact, it is just the opposite. Allowing officers confronted with such flight to stop the fugitive and investigate further is quite consistent with the individual's right to go about his business or to stay put and remain silent in the fact of police questioning.

2. We granted certiorari solely on the question of whether the initial stop was supported by reasonable suspicion. Therefore, we express no opinion as to the lawfulness of the frisk independent of the stop.

Respondent and *amici* also argue that there are innocent reasons for flight from police and that, therefore, flight is not necessarily indicative of ongoing criminal activity. This fact is undoubtedly true, but does not establish a violation of the Fourth Amendment. Even in *Terry*, the conduct justifying the stop was ambiguous and susceptible of an innocent explanation. The officer observed two individuals pacing back and forth in front of a store, peering into the window and periodically conferring. Terry, 392 U.S., at 5–6. All of this conduct was by itself lawful, but it also suggested that the individuals were casing the store for a planned robbery. *Terry* recognized that the officers could detain the individuals to resolve the ambiguity. Id., at 30.

In allowing such detentions, *Terry* accepts the risk that officers may stop innocent people. Indeed, the Fourth Amendment accepts that risk in connection with more drastic police action; persons arrested and detained on probable cause to believe they have committed a crime may turn out to be innocent. The *Terry* stop is a far more minimal intrusion, simply allowing the officer to briefly investigate further. If the officer does not learn facts rising to the level of probable cause, the individual must be allowed to go on his way. But in this case the officers found respondent in possession of a handgun, and arrested him for violation of an Illinois firearms statute. No question of the propriety of the arrest itself is before us.

The judgment of the Supreme Court of Illinois is reversed, and the cause is remanded for further proceedings not inconsistent with this opinion.[*]

---

33. United States v. Brown, 159 F.3d 147 (3d Cir.1998) ("flight combined with other factors may support a warrantless stop and frisk"). Among the other factors noted by the court were that the location was a "high crime" area, that the persons stopped were in the vicinity of a reported crime, and that the streets were otherwise deserted.

In State v. Young, 957 P.2d 681 (Wash.1998), the Supreme Court of Washington rejected *Hodari D.* and said that under state law the test was not whether a person has actually been seized but whether a reasonable person would have felt that he was free to leave. Other state cases following or rejecting *Hodari D.* are cited.

Page 70

35. Ingram v. City of Columbus, 185 F.3d 579 (6th Cir.1999) (circumstances did not justify exception to knock-and-announce rule); United States v. Brown, 251 F.3d 286 (1st Cir.2001) (same).

[*] Justice Stevens wrote an opinion concurring in part and dissenting in part, which Justice Souter, Justice Ginsburg, and Justice Breyer joined.

Page 71

36. A wait of 15 to 20 seconds after a single knock and announcement, during which time there was no denial of admission or other exigent circumstance, is insufficient to authorize a forced entry. United States v. Banks, 282 F.3d 699 (9th Cir.2002).

Page 81

New York v. Harris. See Kirk v. Louisiana, noted in supplement to page 49, above.

Page 88

Graham v. Connor. See Saucier v. Katz, 533 U.S. 194 (2001).

Page 93

Qualified immunity of prison officials is not available for unconstitutional acts if officials had fair warning that acts were unconstitutional, even in a novel factual situation. Hope v. Pelzer, 536 U.S. 730 (2002) (6–3).

CHAPTER 2

STOP (AND FRISK)

Page 117

Florida v. J. L.

529 U.S. 266, 120 S.Ct. 1375, 146 L.Ed.2d 254 (2000).

JUSTICE GINSBURG delivered the opinion of the Court.

The question presented in this case is whether an anonymous tip that a person is carrying a gun is, without more, sufficient to justify a police officer's stop and frisk of that person. We hold that it is not.

I

On October 13, 1995, an anonymous caller reported to the Miami–Dade Police that a young black male standing at a particular bus stop and wearing a plaid shirt was carrying a gun.... So far as the record reveals, there is no audio recording of the tip, and nothing is known about the informant. Sometime after the police received the tip—the record does not say how long—two officers were instructed to respond. They arrived at the bus stop about six minutes later and saw three black males "just hanging out [there]." [App. to Pet. for Cert.], at A–42. One of the three, respondent J. L., was wearing a plaid shirt.... Apart from the tip, the officers had no reason to suspect any of the three of illegal conduct. The officers did not see a firearm, and J. L. made no threatening or otherwise unusual movements.... One of the officers approached J. L., told him to put his hands up on the bus stop, frisked him, and seized a gun from J. L.'s pocket. The second officer frisked the other two individuals, against whom no allegations had been made, and found nothing.

J. L., who was at the time of the frisk "10 days shy of his 16th birth[day]," Tr. of Oral Arg. 6, was charged under state law with carrying a concealed firearm without a license and possessing a firearm while under the age of 18. He moved to suppress the gun as the fruit of an unlawful search, and the trial court granted his motion. The intermediate appellate court reversed, but the Supreme Court of Florida quashed that decision and held the search invalid under the Fourth Amendment. 727 So.2d 204 (1998).

Anonymous tips, the Florida Supreme Court stated, are generally less reliable than tips from known informants and can form the basis for reasonable suspicion only if accompanied by specific indicia of reliability, for example, the correct forecast of a subject's " 'not easily predicted' " movements. Id., at 207 (quoting Alabama v. White, 496 U.S. 325, 332 (1990)). The tip leading to the frisk of J. L., the court observed, provided no such predictions, nor did it contain any other qualifying indicia of reliability.... Two justices dissented. The safety of the police and the public, they maintained, justifies a "firearm exception" to the general rule barring investigatory stops and frisks on the basis of bare-boned anonymous tips. [727 So.2d], at 214–215.

Seeking review in this Court, the State of Florida noted that the decision of the State's Supreme Court conflicts with decisions of other courts declaring similar searches compatible with the Fourth Amendment.... We granted certiorari ... and now affirm the judgment of the Florida Supreme Court.

II

Our "stop and frisk" decisions begin with Terry v. Ohio, 392 U.S. 1 (1968). This Court held in *Terry*

> "[W]here a police officer observes unusual conduct which leads him reasonably to conclude in light of his experience that criminal activity may be afoot and that the persons with whom he is dealing may be armed and presently dangerous, where in the course of investigating this behavior he identifies himself as a policeman and makes reasonable inquiries, and where nothing in the initial stages of the encounter serves to dispel his reasonable fear for his own or others' safety, he is entitled for the protection of himself and others in the area to conduct a carefully limited search of the outer clothing of such persons in an attempt to discover weapons which might be used to assault him." Id., at 30.

In the instant case, the officers' suspicion that J. L. was carrying a weapon arose not from any observations of their own but solely from a call made from an unknown location by an unknown caller. Unlike a tip from a known informant whose reputation can be assessed and who can be held responsible if her allegations turn out to be fabricated, see Adams v. Williams, 407 U.S. 143, 146–147 (1972), "an anonymous tip alone seldom demonstrates the informant's basis of knowledge or veracity," Alabama v. White, 496 U.S., at 329. As we have recognized, however, there are situations in which an anonymous tip, suitably corroborated, exhibits "sufficient indicia of reliability to provide reasonable suspicion to make the investigatory stop." Id., at 327. The question we here confront is whether the tip pointing to J. L. had those indicia of reliability.

In *White*, the police received an anonymous tip asserting that a woman was carrying cocaine and predicting that she would leave an apartment building at a specified time, get into a car matching a particular description, and drive to a named motel.... Standing alone, the tip would not have justified a *Terry* stop.... Only after police observation showed that the informant had accurately predicted the woman's movements, we explained, did it become reasonable to think the tipster had inside knowledge about the suspect and therefore to credit his assertion about the cocaine.... Although the Court held that the suspicion in *White* became reasonable after police surveillance, we regarded the case as borderline. Knowledge about a person's future movements indicates some familiarity with that person's affairs, but having such knowledge does not necessarily imply that the informant knows, in particular, whether that person is carrying hidden contraband. We accordingly classified *White* as a "close case." ...

The tip in the instant case lacked the moderate indicia of reliability present in *White* and essential to the Court's decision in that case. The anonymous call concerning J. L. provided no predictive information and therefore left the police without means to test the informant's knowledge or credibility. That the allegation about the gun turned out to be correct does not suggest that the officers, prior to the frisks, had a reasonable basis for suspecting J. L. of engaging in unlawful conduct: The reasonableness of official suspicion must be measured by what the officers knew before they conducted their search. All the police had to go on in this case was the bare report of an unknown, unaccountable informant who neither explained how he knew about the gun nor supplied any basis for believing he had inside information about J. L. If *White* was a close case on the reliability of anonymous tips, this one surely falls on the other side of the line.

Florida contends that the tip was reliable because its description of the suspect's visible attributes proved accurate: There really was a young black male wearing a plaid shirt at the bus stop.... The United States as *amicus curiae* makes a similar argument, proposing that a stop and frisk should be permitted "when (1) an anonymous tip provides a description of a particular person at a particular location illegally carrying a concealed firearm, (2) police promptly verify the pertinent details of the tip except the existence of the firearm, and (3) there are no factors that cast doubt on the reliability of the tip...." Brief for United States 16. These contentions misapprehend the reliability needed for a tip to justify a *Terry* stop.

An accurate description of a subject's readily observable location and appearance is of course reliable in this limited sense: It will help the police correctly identify the person whom the tipster means to accuse. Such a tip, however, does not show that the tipster has knowledge of concealed criminal activity. The reasonable suspicion here at issue requires that a tip be reliable in its assertion of illegality, not just in its tendency to identify a determinate person....

A second major argument advanced by Florida and the United States as *amicus* is, in essence, that the standard *Terry* analysis should be modified to license a "firearm exception." Under such an exception, a tip alleging an illegal gun would justify a stop and frisk even if the accusation would fail standard pre-search reliability testing. We decline to adopt this position.

Firearms are dangerous, and extraordinary dangers sometimes justify unusual precautions. Our decisions recognize the serious threat that armed criminal pose to public safety; *Terry*'s rule, which permits protective police searches on the basis of reasonable suspicion rather than demanding that officers meet the higher standard of probable cause, responds to this very concern.... But an automatic firearm exception to our established reliability analysis would rove too far. Such an exception would enable any person seeking to harass another to set in motion an intrusive, embarrassing police search of the targeted person simply by placing an anonymous call falsely reporting the target's unlawful carriage of a gun. Nor could one securely confine such an exception to allegations involving firearms. Several Courts of Appeals have held it *per se* foreseeable for people carrying significant amounts of illegal drugs to be carrying guns as well.... If police officers may properly conduct *Terry* frisk on the basis of bare-boned tips about guns, it would be reasonable to maintain under the above-cited decisions that the police should similarly have discretion to frisk based on bare-boned tips about narcotics. As we clarified when we made indicia of reliability critical in *Adams* and *White*, the Fourth Amendment is not so easily satisfied....

The facts of this case do not require us to speculate about the circumstances under which the danger alleged in an anonymous tip might be so great as to justify a search even without a showing of reliability. We do not say, for example, that a report of a person carrying a bomb need bear the indicia of reliability we demand for a report of a person carrying a firearm before the police can constitutionally conduct a frisk. Nor do we hold that public safety officials in quarters where the reasonable expectation of Fourth Amendment privacy is diminished, such as airports ... and schools ... cannot conduct protective searches on the basis of information insufficient to justify searches elsewhere.

Finally, the requirement that an anonymous tip bear standard indicia of reliability in order to justify a stop in no way diminishes a police officer's prerogative, in accord with *Terry*, to conduct a protective search of a person who has already been legitimately stopped. We speak in today's decision only of cases in which the officer's authority to make the initial stop is at issue. In that context, we hold that an anonymous tip lacking indicia of reliability of the kind contemplated in *Adams* and *White* does not justify a stop and frisk whenever and however it alleges the illegal possession of a firearm.

The judgment of the Florida Supreme Court is affirmed.[*]

---

[*] Justice Kennedy wrote a concurring opinion, which Chief Justice Rehnquist joined.

Page 119

57. Bond v. United States, 529 U.S. 334 (2000) (7–2) (law officer's manipulation of luggage of bus passenger, which passenger had placed on rack above his seat, was a search that violated the passenger's rights under the Fourth Amendment).

Place is distinguished in B.C. v. Plumas Unified School District, 192 F.3d 1260 (9th Cir.1999), in which school authorities required students to pass in front of a dog trained to sniff for drugs. Saying that a dog sniff of one's person is offensive, the court held that the sniff violated the plaintiff's reasonable expectation of privacy and constituted a search.

Page 123

62. See supplement to page 60, Note 33, above.

Page 124

See United States v. Sigmond-Ballesteros, 285 F.3d 1117 (9th Cir.2002) (rejecting various alleged grounds for reasonable suspicion justifying stop of motor vehicle).

Page 129

Dickerson. United States v. Mattarolo, 209 F.3d 1153 (9th Cir.2000) ("plain feel" upheld).

Page 137

For a rare case in which a court concluded that an officer's asserted basis for an investigative detention (in this case of a motor home) beyond a traffic stop was inadequate, see United States v. Salzano, 149 F.3d 1238 (10th Cir.1998).

Page 139

United States v. Washington, 151 F.3d 1354 (11th Cir.1998) (officer's failure to advise bus passengers that they could refuse consent to search made defendant's consent ineffective, in circumstances of the case).

Page 145

United States v. Drayton

536 U.S. 194, 122 S.Ct. 2105, 153 L.Ed.2d 242 (2002).

■ JUSTICE KENNEDY delivered the opinion of the Court.

The Fourth Amendment permits police officers to approach bus passengers at random to ask questions and to request their consent to searches, provided a reasonable person would understand that he or she is free to refuse. Florida v. Bostick, 501 U.S. 429 (1991). This case requires us to determine whether officers must advise bus passengers during these encounters of their right not to cooperate.

I

On February 4, 1999, respondents Christopher Drayton and Clifton Brown, Jr., were traveling on a Greyhound bus en route from Ft. Lauderdale, Florida, to Detroit, Michigan. The bus made a scheduled stop in Tallahassee, Florida. The passengers were required to disembark so the bus could be refueled and cleaned. As the passengers reboarded, the driver checked their tickets and then left to complete paperwork inside the terminal. As he left, the driver allowed three members of the Tallahassee Police Department to board the bus as part of a routine drug and weapons interdiction effort. The officers were dressed in plain clothes and carried concealed weapons and visible badges.

Once onboard Officer Hoover knelt on the driver's seat and faced the rear of the bus. He could observe the passengers and ensure the safety of the two other officers without blocking the aisle or otherwise obstructing the bus exit. Officers Lang and Blackburn went to the rear of the bus. Blackburn remained stationed there, facing forward. Lang worked his way toward the front of the bus, speaking with individual passengers as he went. He asked the passengers about their travel plans and sought to match passengers with luggage in the overhead racks. To avoid blocking the aisle, Lang stood next to or just behind each passenger with whom he spoke.

According to Lang's testimony, passengers who declined to cooperate with him or who chose to exit the bus at any time would have been allowed to do so without argument. In Lang's experience, however, most people are willing to cooperate. Some passengers go so far as to commend the police for their efforts to ensure the safety of their travel. Lang could recall five to six instances in the previous year in which passengers had declined to have their luggage searched. It also was common for passengers to leave the bus for a cigarette or a snack while the officers were on board. Lang sometimes informed passengers of their right to refuse to cooperate. On the day in question, however, he did not.

Respondents were seated next to each other on the bus. Drayton was in the aisle seat, Brown in the seat next to the window. Lang approached respondents from the rear and leaned over Drayton's shoulder. He held up his badge long enough for respondents to identify him as a police officer. With his face 12-to-18 inches away from Drayton's, Lang spoke in a voice just loud enough for respondents to hear:

> "I'm Investigator Lang with the Tallahassee Police Department. We're conducting bus interdiction [sic], attempting to deter drugs and illegal weapons being transported on the bus. Do you have any bags on the bus?" App. 55.

Both respondents pointed to a single green bag in the overhead luggage rack. Lang asked, "Do you mind if I check it?," and Brown responded, "Go ahead." Id., at 56. Lang handed the bag to Officer Blackburn to check. The bag contained no contraband.

Officer Lang noticed that both respondents were wearing heavy jackets and baggy pants despite the warm weather. In Lang's experience drug traffickers often use baggy clothing to conceal weapons or narcotics. The officer thus asked Brown if he had any weapons or drugs in his possession. And he asked Brown: "Do you mind if I check your person?" Brown answered, "Sure," and cooperated by leaning up in his seat, pulling a cell phone out of his pocket, and opening up his jacket. Id., at 61. Lang reached across Drayton and patted down Brown's jacket and pockets, including his waist area, sides, and upper thighs. In both thigh areas, Lang detected hard objects similar to drug packages detected on other occasions. Lang arrested and handcuffed Brown. Officer Hoover escorted Brown from the bus.

Lang then asked Drayton, "Mind if I check you?" Id., at 65. Drayton responded by lifting his hands about eight inches from his legs. Lang conducted a pat-down of Drayton's thighs and detected hard objects similar to those found on Brown. He arrested Drayton and escorted him from the bus. A further search revealed that respondents had duct-taped plastic bundles of powder cocaine between several pairs of their boxer shorts. Brown possessed three bundles containing 483 grams of cocaine. Drayton possessed two bundles containing 295 grams of cocaine.

Respondents were charged with conspiring to distribute cocaine, in violation of 21 U.S.C. §§ 841(a)(1) and 846, and with possessing cocaine with intent to distribute it, in violation of § 841(a)(1). They moved to suppress the cocaine, arguing that the consent to the pat-down search was invalid. Following a hearing at which only Officer Lang testified, the United States District Court for the Northern District of Florida denied their motions to suppress. . . .

The Court of Appeals for the Eleventh Circuit reversed and remanded with instructions to grant respondents' motions to suppress. . . .

We granted certiorari. . . . The respondents, we conclude, were not seized and their consent to the search was voluntary; and we reverse.

II

Law enforcement officers do not violate the Fourth Amendment's prohibition of unreasonable seizures merely by approaching individuals on the street or in other public places and putting questions to them if they are willing to listen. . . . Even when law enforcement officers have no basis for suspecting a particular individual, they may pose questions, ask for identification, and request consent to search luggage—provided they do not induce cooperation by coercive means. . . . If a reasonable person would feel free to terminate the encounter, then he or she has not been seized.

The Court has addressed on a previous occasion the specific question of drug interdiction efforts on buses. In *Bostick*, two police officers requested a bus passenger's consent to a search of his luggage. The passenger agreed, and the resulting search revealed cocaine in his suitcase. The Florida Supreme Court suppressed the cocaine. In doing so it adopted a per se rule that due to the cramped confines onboard a bus the act of questioning would deprive a person of his or her freedom of movement and so constitute a seizure under the Fourth Amendment.

This Court reversed. *Bostick* first made it clear that for the most part per se rules are inappropriate in the Fourth Amendment context. The proper inquiry necessitates a consideration of "all the circumstances surrounding the encounter." Id., at 439. The Court noted next that the traditional rule, which states that a seizure does not occur so long as a reasonable person would feel free "to disregard the police and go about his business," California v. Hodari D., 499 U.S. 621, 628 (1991), is not an accurate measure of the coercive effect of a bus encounter. A passenger may not want to get off a bus if there is a risk it will depart before the opportunity to reboard. . . . A bus rider's movements are confined in this sense, but this is the natural result of choosing to take the bus; it says nothing about whether the police conduct is coercive. . . . The proper inquiry "is whether a reasonable person would feel free to decline the officers' requests or otherwise terminate the encounter." [*Bostick*, 501 U.S.] at 436. Finally, the Court rejected Bostick's argument that he must have been seized because no reasonable person would consent to a search of luggage containing drugs. The reasonable person test, the Court explained, is objective and "presupposes an *innocent* person." Id., at 437–438.

In light of the limited record, *Bostick* refrained from deciding whether a seizure occurred. . . . The Court, however, identified two factors "particularly worth noting" on remand. Id., at 432. First, although it was obvious that an officer was armed, he did not remove the gun from its pouch or use it in a threatening way. Second, the officer advised the passenger that he could refuse consent to the search. . . .

Relying upon this latter factor, the Eleventh Circuit has adopted what is in effect a per se rule that evidence obtained during suspicionless drug interdiction efforts aboard buses must be suppressed unless the officers have advised passengers of their right not to cooperate and to refuse consent to a search. . . .

. . .

Applying the *Bostick* framework to the facts of this particular case, we conclude that the police did not seize respondents when they boarded the bus and began questioning passengers. The officers gave the passengers no reason to believe that they were required to answer the officers' questions. When Officer Lang approached respondents, he did not brandish a weapon or make any intimidating movements. He left the aisle free so that respondents could exit. He spoke to passengers one by one and in a polite, quiet voice. Nothing he said would suggest to a reasonable person that he or she was barred from leaving the bus or otherwise terminating the encounter.

. . . There was no application of force, no intimidating movement, no overwhelming show of force, no brandishing of weapons, no blocking of exits, no threat, no command, not even an authoritative tone of voice. It is beyond question that had this encounter occurred on the street, it would be constitutional. The fact that an encounter takes place on a bus does not on its own transform standard police questioning of citizens into an illegal seizure. . . . Indeed, because many fellow passengers are present to witness officers' conduct, a reasonable person may feel even more secure in his or her decision not to cooperate with police on a bus than in other circumstances.

Respondents make much of the fact that Officer Lang displayed his badge. In Florida v. Rodriguez, 469 U.S., at 5–6, however, the Court rejected the claim that the defendant was seized when an officer approached him in an airport, showed him his badge, and asked him to answer some questions. Likewise, in INS v. Delgado, 466 U.S. 210, 212–213 (1984), the Court held that INS agents' wearing badges and questioning workers in a factory did not constitute a seizure. And while neither Lang nor his colleagues were in uniform or visibly armed, those factors should have little weight in the analysis. Officers are often required to wear uniforms and in many circumstances this is cause for assurance, not discomfort. Much the same can be said for wearing sidearms. That most law enforcement officers are armed is a fact well known to the public. The presence of a holstered firearm thus is unlikely to contribute to the coerciveness of the encounter absent active brandishing of the weapon.

Officer Hoover's position at the front of the bus also does not tip the scale in respondents' favor. Hoover did nothing to intimidate passengers, and he said nothing to suggest that people could not exit and indeed he left the aisle clear. . . .

Finally, the fact that in Officer Lang's experience only a few passengers have refused to cooperate does not suggest that a reasonable person would not feel free to terminate the bus encounter. In Lang's experience it was common for passengers to leave the bus for a cigarette or a snack while the officers were questioning passengers. . . . And of more importance, bus passengers answer officers' questions and otherwise cooperate not because of coercion but because the passengers know that their participation enhances their own safety and the safety of those around them. . . .

Drayton contends that even if Brown's cooperation with the officers was consensual, Drayton was seized because no reasonable person would feel free to terminate the encounter with the officers after Brown had been arrested.... The arrest of one person does not mean that everyone around him has been seized by police. If anything, Brown's arrest should have put Drayton on notice of the consequences of continuing the encounter by answering the officers' questions. Even after arresting Brown, Lang addressed Drayton in a polite manner and provided him with no indication that he was required to answer Lang's questions.

We turn now from the question whether respondents were seized to whether they were subjected to an unreasonable search, i.e., whether their consent to the suspicionless search was involuntary. In circumstances such as these, where the question of voluntariness pervades both the search and seizure inquiries, the respective analyses turn on very similar facts. And, as the facts above suggest, respondents' consent to the search of their luggage and their persons was voluntary. Nothing Officer Lang said indicated a command to consent to the search. Rather, when respondents informed Lang that they had a bag on the bus, he asked for their permission to check it. And when Lang requested to search Brown and Drayton's persons, he asked first if they objected, thus indicating to a reasonable person that he or she was free to refuse. Even after arresting Brown, Lang provided Drayton with no indication that he was required to consent to a search. To the contrary, Lang asked for Drayton's permission to search him ("Mind if I check you?"), and Drayton agreed.

The Court has rejected in specific terms the suggestion that police officers must always inform citizens of their right to refuse when seeking permission to conduct a warrantless consent search.... Nor do this Court's decisions suggest that even though there are no per se rules, a presumption of invalidity attaches if a citizen consented without explicit notification that he or she was free to refuse to cooperate. Instead, the Court has repeated that the totality of the circumstances must control, without giving extra weight to the absence of this type of warning.... Although Officer Lang did not inform respondents of their right to refuse the search, he did request permission to search, and the totality of the circumstances indicates that their consent was voluntary, so the searches were reasonable.

In a society based on law, the concept of agreement and consent should be given a weight and dignity of its own. Police officers act in full accord with the law when they ask citizens for consent. It reinforces the rule of law for the citizen to advise the police of his or her wishes and for the police to act in reliance on that understanding. When this exchange takes place, it dispels inferences of coercion.

We need not ask the alternative question whether, after the arrest of Brown, there were grounds for a *Terry* stop and frisk of Drayton ... though this may have been the case. It was evident that Drayton and Brown were traveling together—Officer Lang observed the pair reboarding the bus together; they were each dressed in heavy, baggy clothes that were ill-suited for the day's warm temperatures; they were seated together on the bus; and they each claimed responsibility for the single piece of green carry-on luggage. Once Lang had identified Brown as carrying what he believed to be narcotics, he may have had reasonable suspicion to conduct a *Terry* stop and frisk on Drayton as well. That question, however, has not been presented to us. The fact the officers may have had reasonable suspicion does not prevent them from relying on a citizen's consent to the search. It would be a paradox, and one most puzzling to law enforcement officials and courts alike, were we to say, after holding that Brown's consent was voluntary, that Drayton's consent was ineffectual simply because the police at that point had more compelling grounds to detain him. After taking Brown into custody, the officers were entitled to continue to proceed on the basis of consent and to ask for Drayton's cooperation.

The judgment of the Court of Appeals is reversed, and the case is remanded for further proceedings consistent with this opinion.

■ JUSTICE SOUTER, with whom JUSTICE STEVENS and JUSTICE GINSBURG join, dissenting.

Anyone who travels by air today submits to searches of the person and luggage as a condition of boarding the aircraft. It is universally accepted that such intrusions are necessary to hedge against risks that, nowadays, even small children understand. The commonplace precautions of air travel have not, thus far, been justified for ground transportation, however, and no such conditions have been placed on passengers getting on trains or buses. There is therefore an air of unreality about the Court's explanation that bus passengers consent to searches of their luggage to "enhanc[e] their own safety and the safety of those around them." Ante, at 205. Nor are the other factual assessments underlying the Court's conclusion in favor of the Government more convincing.

The issue we took to review is whether the police's examination of the bus passengers, including respondents, amounted to a suspicionless seizure under the Fourth Amendment. If it did, any consent to search was plainly invalid as a product of the illegal seizure. . . .

Florida v. Bostick, 501 U.S. 429 (1991), established the framework for determining whether the bus passengers were seized in the constitutional sense. In that case, we rejected the position that police questioning of bus passengers was a per se seizure, and held instead that the issue of seizure was to be resolved under an objective test considering all circumstances: whether a reasonable passenger would have felt "free to decline the officers' requests or otherwise terminate the encounter," id., at 436. We thus applied to a bus passenger the more general criterion, whether the person questioned was free "to ignore the police presence and go about his business," id., at 437 (quoting Michigan v. Chesternut, 486 U.S. 567, 569 (1988)).

Before applying the standard in this case, it may be worth getting some perspective from different sets of facts. A perfect example of police conduct that supports no colorable claim of seizure is the act of an officer who simply goes up to a pedestrian on the street and asks him a question.... A pair of officers questioning a pedestrian, without more, would presumably support the same conclusion. Now consider three officers, one of whom stands behind the pedestrian, another at his side toward the open sidewalk, with the third addressing questions to the pedestrian a foot or two from his face. Finally, consider the same scene in a narrow alley. On such barebones facts, one may not be able to say a seizure occurred, even in the last case, but one can say without qualification that the atmosphere of the encounters differed significantly from the first to the last examples. In the final instance there is every reason to believe that the pedestrian would have understood, to his considerable discomfort, what Justice Stewart described as the "threatening presence of several officers," United States v. Mendenhall, 446 U.S. 544, 554 (1980) (opinion of Stewart, J.). The police not only carry legitimate authority but also exercise power free from immediate check, and when the attention of several officers is brought to bear on one civilian the imbalance of immediate power is unmistakable. We all understand this, as well as we understand that a display of power rising to Justice Stewart's "threatening" level may overbear a normal person's ability to act freely, even in the absence of explicit commands or the formalities of detention. As common as this understanding is, however, there is little sign of it in the Court's opinion. My own understanding of the relevant facts and their significance follows.

When the bus in question made its scheduled stop in Tallahassee, the passengers were required to disembark while the vehicle was cleaned and refueled.... When the passengers returned, they gave their tickets to the driver, who kept them and then left himself, after giving three police officers permission to board the bus in his absence.... Although they were not in uniform, the officers displayed badges and identified themselves as police. One stationed himself in the driver's seat by the door at the front, facing back to observe the passengers. The two others went to the rear, from which they worked their way forward, with one of them speaking to passengers, the other backing him up.... They necessarily addressed the passengers at very close range; the aisle was only fifteen inches wide, and each seat only eighteen. The quarters were cramped further by the overhead rack, nineteen inches above the top of the passenger seats. The passenger by the window could not have stood up straight ... and the face of the nearest officer was only a foot or eighteen inches from the face of the nearest passenger being addressed.... During the exchanges, the officers looked down, and the passengers had to look up if they were to face the police. The officer asking the questions spoke quietly. He prefaced his requests for permission to search luggage and do a body patdown by identifying himself by name as a police investigator "conducting bus interdiction" and saying, " 'We would like for your cooperation. Do you have any luggage on the bus?' " [App.] at 82.

Thus, for reasons unexplained, the driver with the tickets entitling the passengers to travel had yielded his custody of the bus and its seated travelers to three police officers, whose authority apparently superseded the driver's own. The officers took control of the entire passenger compartment, one stationed at the door keeping surveillance of all the occupants, the others working forward from the back. With one officer right behind him and the other one forward, a third officer accosted each passenger at quarters extremely close and so cramped that as many as half the passengers could not even have stood to face the speaker. None was asked whether he was willing to converse with the police or to take part in the enquiry. Instead the officer said the police were "conducting bus interdiction," in the course of which they "would like ... cooperation." Ibid. The reasonable inference was that the "interdiction" was not a consensual exercise, but one the police would carry out whatever the circumstances; that they would prefer "cooperation" but would not let the lack of it stand in their way. There was no contrary indication that day, since no passenger had refused the cooperation requested, and there was no reason for any passenger to believe that the driver would return and the trip resume until the police were satisfied. The scene was set and an atmosphere of obligatory participation was established by this introduction. Later requests to search prefaced with "Do you mind ... " would naturally have been understood in the terms with which the encounter began.

It is very hard to imagine that either Brown or Drayton would have believed that he stood to lose nothing if he refused to cooperate with the police, or that he had any free choice to ignore the police altogether. No reasonable passenger could have believed that, only an uncomprehending one. It is neither here nor there that the interdiction was conducted by three officers, not one, as a safety precaution.... The fact was that there were three, and when Brown and Drayton were called upon to respond, each one was presumably conscious of an officer in front watching, one at his side questioning him, and one behind for cover, in case he became unruly, perhaps, or "cooperation" was not forthcoming. The situation is much like the one in the alley, with civilians in close quarters, unable to move effectively, being told their cooperation is expected. While I am not prepared to say that no bus interrogation and search can pass the *Bostick* test without a warning that passengers are free to say no, the facts here surely required more from the officers than a quiet tone of voice. A police officer who is certain to get his way has no need to shout.

It is true of course that the police testified that a bus passenger sometimes says no ... but that evidence does nothing to cast the facts here in a different light. We have no way of knowing the circumstances in which a passenger elsewhere refused a request; maybe that has happened only when the police have told passengers they had a right to refuse (as the officers sometimes advised them).... Nor is it fairly possible to see the facts of this case differently by recalling INS v. Delgado, 466 U.S. 210 (1984), as precedent.... In this case ... Brown and Drayton were seemingly pinned-in by the officers and the customary course of events was stopped flat. The bus was going nowhere, and with one officer in the driver's seat, it was reasonable to suppose no passenger would tend to his own business until the officers were ready to let him.

In any event, I am less concerned to parse this case against *Delgado* than to apply *Bostick*'s totality of circumstances test, and to ask whether a passenger would reasonably have felt free to end his encounter with the three officers by saying no and ignoring them thereafter. In my view the answer is clear. The Court's contrary conclusion tells me that the majority cannot see what Justice Stewart saw, and I respectfully dissent.

Narcotics agents became suspicious of the defendant when they observed him in a bus terminal and watched as he boarded a bus and placed his bag in an overhead compartment. When the bus was scheduled to depart, they boarded the bus and announced that they were conducting a routine narcotics investigation and would like to talk to the passengers but that anyone was free to leave. When they talked to the defendant he said that he had no carry-on baggage. They removed the bag that he had carried on and asked if anyone owned it. When the bag was not claimed, they removed it and opened it. It contained narcotics.

The court concluded that the defendant had abandoned the bag but that the abandonment was involuntary and the result of an unlawful seizure. It said that the agents' announcement and conduct indicated to passengers that they had only two choices: to cooperate with the agents or to get off the bus, which would itself have created suspicion. In view of all the circumstances, the court concluded that the defendant had been seized. United States v. Stephens, 206 F.3d 914 (9th Cir.2000).

Page 146

66. United States v. Burton, 228 F.3d 524 (4th Cir.2000) (officer can initiate "police-citizen contact" without reasonable suspicion but cannot rely solely on person's refusal to cooperate as basis for reasonable suspicion justifying frisk).

Page 154

United States v. Yang, 286 F.3d 940 (7th Cir.2002) ("extended border search" at international airport).

Page 155

United States v. Montero-Camargo, 208 F.3d 1122 (9th Cir.2000).

City of Indianapolis v. Edmond

531 U.S. 32, 121 S.Ct. 447, 148 L.Ed.2d 333 (2000).

■ JUSTICE O'CONNOR delivered the opinion of the Court.

In Michigan Dept. of State Police v. Sitz, 496 U.S. 444 (1990), and United States v. Martinez-Fuerte, 428 U.S. 543 (1976), we held that brief, suspicionless seizures at highway checkpoints for the purposes of combating drunk driving and intercepting illegal immigrants were constitutional. We now consider the constitutionality of a highway checkpoint program whose primary purpose is the discovery and interdiction of illegal narcotics.

I

In August 1998, the city of Indianapolis began to operate vehicle checkpoints on Indianapolis roads in an effort to interdict unlawful drugs. The city conducted six such roadblocks between August and November that year, stopping 1,161 vehicles and arresting 104 motorists. Fifty-five arrests were for drug-related crimes, while 49 were for offenses unrelated to drugs.... The overall "hit rate" of the program was thus approximately nine percent.

The parties stipulated to the facts concerning the operation of the checkpoints by the Indianapolis Police Department (IPD) for purposes of the preliminary injunction proceedings instituted below. At each checkpoint location, the police stop a predetermined number of vehicles. Approximately 30 officers are stationed at the checkpoint. Pursuant to written directives issued by the chief of police, at least one officer approaches the vehicle, advises the driver that he or she is being stopped briefly at a drug checkpoint, and asks the driver to produce a license and registration. The officer also looks for signs of impairment and conducts an open-view examination of the vehicle from the outside. A narcotics-detection dog walks around the outside of each stopped vehicle.

The directives instruct the officers that they may conduct a search only by consent or based on the appropriate quantum of particularized suspicion. The officers must conduct each stop in the same manner until particularized suspicion develops, and the officers have no discretion to stop any vehicle out of sequence. The city agreed in the stipulation to operate the checkpoints in such a way as to ensure that the total duration of each stop, absent reasonable suspicion or probable cause, would be five minutes or less.

The affidavit of Indianapolis Police Sergeant Marshall DePew, although it is technically outside the parties' stipulation, provides further insight concerning the operation of the checkpoints. According to Sergeant DePew, checkpoint locations are selected weeks in advance based on such considerations as area crime statistics and traffic flow. The checkpoints are generally operated during daylight hours and are identified with lighted signs reading, "NARCOTICS CHECKPOINT ___ MILE AHEAD, NAR-

COTICS K–9 IN USE, BE PREPARED TO STOP." App. to Pet. for Cert. 57a. Once a group of cars has been stopped, other traffic proceeds without interruption until all the stopped cars have been processed or diverted for further processing. Sergeant DePew also stated that the average stop for a vehicle not subject to further processing lasts two to three minutes or less.

Respondents James Edmond and Joell Palmer were each stopped at a narcotics checkpoint in late September 1998. Respondents then filed a lawsuit on behalf of themselves and the class of all motorists who had been stopped or were subject to being stopped in the future at the Indianapolis drug checkpoints. Respondents claimed that the roadblocks violated the Fourth Amendment of the United States Constitution and the search and seizure provision of the Indiana Constitution....

Respondents then moved for a preliminary injunction.... The United States District Court for the Southern District of Indiana ... denied the motion for a preliminary injunction, holding that the checkpoint program did not violate the Fourth Amendment.... A divided panel of the United States Court of Appeals for the Seventh Circuit reversed, holding that the checkpoints contravened the Fourth Amendment.... We granted certiorari ... and now affirm.

II

The Fourth Amendment requires that searches and seizures be reasonable. A search or seizure is ordinarily unreasonable in the absence of individualized suspicion of wrongdoing.... While such suspicion is not an "irreducible" component of reasonableness, *Martinez-Fuerte*, 428 U.S., at 561, we have recognized only limited circumstances in which the usual rule does not apply. For example, we have upheld certain regimes of suspicionless searches where the program was designed to serve "special needs, beyond the normal need for law enforcement." See, e.g., Vernonia School Dist. 47J v. Acton, 515 U.S. 646 (1995) (random drug testing of student athletes); National Treasury Employees Union v. Von Raab, 489 U.S. 656 (1989) (drug tests for United States Customs Service employees seeking transfer or promotion to certain positions); Skinner v. Railway Labor Executives' Assn., 489 U.S. 602 (1989) (drug and alcohol tests for railway employees involved in train accidents or found to be in violation of particular safety regulations). We have also allowed searches for certain administrative purposes without particularized suspicion of misconduct, provided that those searches are appropriately limited. See., e.g., New York v. Burger, 482 U.S. 691, 702–704 (1987) (warrantless administrative inspection of premises of "closely regulated" business); Michigan v. Tyler, 436 U.S. 499, 507–509, 511–512 (1978) (administrative inspection of fire-damaged premises to determine cause of blaze); Camara v. Municipal Court of City and County of San Francisco, 387 U.S. 523, 534–539 (1967) (administrative inspection to ensure compliance with city housing code).

We have also upheld brief, suspicionless seizures of motorists at a fixed Border Patrol checkpoint designed to intercept illegal aliens, *Martinez-Fuerte*, supra, and at a sobriety checkpoint aimed at removing drunk drivers from the road, Michigan Dept. of State Police v. Sitz, 496 U.S. 444 (1990). In addition, in Delaware v. Prouse, 440 U.S. 648 (663) (1979), we suggested that a similar type of roadblock with the purpose of verifying drivers' licenses and vehicle registrations would be permissible. In none of these cases, however, did we indicate approval of a checkpoint program whose primary purpose was to detect evidence of ordinary criminal wrongdoing.

. . .

III

It is well established that a vehicle stop at a highway checkpoint effectuates a seizure within the meaning of the Fourth Amendment.... The fact that officers walk a narcotics-detection dog around the exterior of each car at the Indianapolis checkpoints does not transform the seizure into a search.... Rather, what principally distinguishes these checkpoints from those we have previously approved is their primary purpose.

As petitioners concede, the Indianapolis checkpoint program unquestionably has the primary purpose of interdicting illegal narcotics....

We have never approved a checkpoint program whose primary purpose was to detect evidence of ordinary criminal wrongdoing. Rather, our checkpoint cases have recognized only limited exceptions to the general rule that a seizure must be accompanied by some measure of individualized suspicion.... [E]ach of the checkpoint programs that we have approved was designed primarily to serve purposes closely related to the problems of policing the border or the necessity of ensuring roadway safety. Because the primary purpose of the Indianapolis narcotics checkpoint program is to uncover evidence of ordinary criminal wrongdoing, the program contravenes the Fourth Amendment.

Petitioners propose several ways in which the narcotics-detection purpose of the instant checkpoint program may instead resemble the primary purposes of the checkpoints in *Sitz* and *Martinez-Fuerte*. Petitioners state that the checkpoints in those cases had the same ultimate purpose of arresting those suspected of committing crimes.... Securing the border and apprehending drunk drivers are, of course, law enforcement activities, and law enforcement officers employ arrests and criminal prosecutions in pursuit of these goals.... If we were to rest the case at this high level of generality, there would be little check on the ability of the authorities to construct roadblocks for almost any conceivable law enforcement purpose. Without drawing the line at roadblocks designed primarily to serve the general interest in crime control, the Fourth Amendment would do little to prevent such intrusions from becoming a routine part of American life.

Petitioners also emphasize the severe and intractable nature of the drug problem as justification for the checkpoint program.... There is no doubt that traffic in illegal narcotics creates social harms of the first magnitude.... The law enforcement problems that the drug trade creates likewise remain daunting and complex, particularly in light of the myriad forms of spin-off crime that it spawns.... The same can be said of various other illegal activities, if only to a lesser degree. But the gravity of the threat alone cannot be dispositive of questions concerning what means law enforcement officers may employ to pursue a given purpose. Rather, in determining whether individualized suspicion is required, we must consider the nature of the interest threatened and their connection to the particular law enforcement practices at issue. We are particularly reluctant to recognize exceptions to the general rule of individualized suspicion where governmental authorities primarily pursue their general crime control ends.

Nor can the narcotics-interdiction purpose of the checkpoints be rationalized in terms of a highway safety concern....

. . .

The primary purpose of the Indianapolis narcotics checkpoints is in the end to advance "the general interest in crime control," *Prouse*, 440 U.S., at 659, n.18. We decline to suspend the usual requirement of individualized suspicion where the police seek to employ a checkpoint primarily for the ordinary enterprise of investigating crimes. We cannot sanction stops justified only by the generalized and ever-present possibility that interrogation and inspection may reveal that any given motorist has committed some crime.

Of course, there are circumstances that may justify a law enforcement checkpoint where the primary purpose would otherwise, but for some emergency, relate to ordinary crime control. For example, as the Court of Appeals noted, the Fourth Amendment would almost certainly permit an appropriately tailored roadblock set up to thwart an imminent terrorist attack or to catch a dangerous criminal who is likely to flee by way of a particular route.... The exigencies created by these scenarios are far removed from the circumstances under which authorities might simply stop cars as a matter of course to see if there just happens to be a felon leaving the jurisdiction. While we do not limit the purposes that may justify a checkpoint program to any rigid set of categories, we decline to approve a program whose primary purpose is ultimately indistinguishable from the general interest in crime control.

. . .

Petitioners argue that the Indianapolis checkpoint program is justified by its lawful secondary purposes of keeping impaired motorists off the road and verifying licenses and registrations.... If this were the case, however, law enforcement authorities would be able to establish checkpoints for virtually any purpose so long as they also included a license or sobriety check. For this reason, we examine the available evidence to determine the primary purpose of the checkpoint program. While we recognize the challenges inherent in a purpose inquiry, courts routinely engage in this enterprise in many areas of constitutional jurisprudence as a means of sifting abusive governmental conduct from that which is lawful.... As a result, a program driven by an impermissible purpose may be proscribed while a program impelled by licit purposes is permitted, even though the challenged conduct may be outwardly similar. While reasonableness under the Fourth Amendment is predominantly an objective inquiry, our special needs and administrative search cases demonstrate that purpose is often relevant when suspicionless intrusions pursuant to a general scheme are at issue.[2]

It goes without saying that our holding today does nothing to alter the constitutional status of the sobriety and border checkpoints that we approved in *Sitz* and *Martinez-Fuerte*, or of the type of traffic checkpoint that we suggested would be lawful in *Prouse*....

Our holding also does not affect the validity of border searches or searches at places like airports and government buildings, where the need for such measures to ensure public safety can be particularly acute. Nor does our opinion speak to other intrusions aimed primarily at purposes beyond the general interest in crime control. Our holding also does not impair the ability of police officers to act appropriately upon information that they properly learn during a checkpoint stop justified by a lawful primary purpose, even where such action may result in the arrest of a motorist for an offense unrelated to that purpose. Finally, we caution that the purpose inquiry in this context is to be conducted only at the programmatic level and is not an invitation to probe the minds of individual officers acting at the scene....

Because the primary purpose of the Indianapolis checkpoint program is ultimately indistinguishable from the general interest in crime control, the checkpoints violate the Fourth Amendment. The judgment of the Court of Appeals is accordingly affirmed.[*]

---

2. Because petitioners concede that the primary purpose of the Indianapolis checkpoints is narcotics detection, we need not decide whether the State may establish a checkpoint program with the primary purpose of checking licenses or driver sobriety and a secondary purpose of interdicting narcotics. Specifically, we express no view on the question whether police may expand the scope of a license or sobriety checkpoint seizure in order to detect the presence of drugs in a stopped car....

[*] Chief Justice Rehnquist wrote a dissenting opinion, which Justice Thomas joined and part I of which Justice Scalia joined. Justice Thomas also wrote a dissenting opinion.

CHAPTER 3

SEARCH

Page 162

United States v. Thomas, 263 F.3d 805 (8th Cir.2001) (warrant invalid because it contained incorrect address; good faith exception applied).

Page 165

79. The exclusionary rule does not apply in parole revocation hearings. Pennsylvania Board of Probation and Parole v. Scott, 524 U.S. 357 (1998) (5–4). The majority reasoned that application of the exclusionary rule in such hearings "would provide only minimal deterrence benefits" and "is incompatible with the traditionally flexible administrative procedures of parole revocation," id. at 364, 365. Justice Souter, dissenting, observed that "without a suppression remedy in revocation proceedings, there will often be no influence capable of deterring Fourth Amendment violations when parole revocation is a possible response to new crime." Id. at 379.

Page 179

85. A warrantless search supported by reasonable suspicion, of the premises of a person sentenced to probation for a drug offense, whose probation was expressly conditional on his submission to a search by a law enforcement officer at any time, is valid. United States v. Knights, 534 U.S. 112 (2001). The Court said that viewing the totality of the circumstances, the fact that a person is on probation alters the balance by which the reasonableness of a search is assessed. It both increases the likelihood that the person is violating the law and, as a form of criminal punishment, somewhat reduces the person's liberty and, therefore, his expectation of privacy.

A person's status as a parolee does not wholly defeat his legitimate expectation of privacy in his own home, even if, as a mandatory condition of parole, he has signed a blanket waiver of objection to any search. A search of his home without reasonable suspicion to believe that evidence of criminal activity would be found violates the Fourth Amendment. United States v. Crawford, 323 F.3d 700 (9th Cir.2003).

See United States v. Reyes, 283 F.3d 446 (2d Cir.2002), stating that a person on probation has a "significantly diminished" expectation of privacy with respect to supervision by a probation officer and rejecting the "stalking horse'' theory that if a probation officer acts at the behest of law enforcement authorities, the usual Fourth Amendment standards apply.

In Anderson v. Commonwealth, 507 S.E.2d 339 (Va.1998), the court held that a defendant's waiver of ''his Fourth Amendment right against unreasonable searches and seizures for a period of one year from the date of sentencing,'' as part of a plea agreement, was valid.

Page 181

A person's consent to a general search of a computer does not authorize a search of the files of another joint user of the computer, whose files are protected by a password to which the consenting person does not have access. Trulock v. Freeh, 275 F.3d 391 (4th Cir.2001). The court likened the protected files to a locked footlocker.

Page 182

89. Cf. United States v. Wesela, 223 F.3d 656 (7th Cir.2000).

Matlock. United States v. Flores, 172 F.3d 695 (9th Cir.1999) (consent of cotenant effective despite nonconsent of present cotenant).

Page 183

United States v. Rith, 164 F.3d 1323 (10th Cir.1999) (consent of co-occupant is valid despite objection of *present* nonconsenting occupant).

Page 184

United States v. Rith, 164 F.3d 1323 (10th Cir.1999) (parent had sufficient control over entire house to give valid consent to search of adult child's bedroom).

See State v. Kieffer, 577 N.W.2d 352 (Wis.1998) (father-in-law lacked authority to consent to search of premises in house owned by him, in circumstances of case).

Page 192

Rule 41. Rule 41 has been amended. As amended, the rule includes a provision, conforming to a statute, providing for the issuance of warrants outside a magistrate judge's district in cases involving terrorism.

For the text of the rule as amended, including stylistic changes, see Appendix.

Page 194

Rule 41(d). In the absence of special circumstances, Rule 41(d) requires an officer executing a warrant to give a copy of the warrant to the person whose premises are to be searched, if present, before the search is executed. United States v. Gantt, 179 F.3d 782 (9th Cir.1999) (evidence properly suppressed).

Page 211

103. In Burchett v. Kiefer, 310 F.3d 937 (6th Cir.2002), the court, applying Michigan v. Summers, held that police executing a search warrant may detain a person who approaches but does not go on the property and flees when the police tell him to get on the ground, for the duration of the search.

Page 212

It is a violation of the Fourth Amendment for police who are executing a search warrant to allow members of the media or other persons to accompany them into the premises to be searched, if their presence is not in aid of execution of the warrant. Wilson v. Layne, 526 U.S. 603 (1999). The Court held also, however, that since the law was not clearly established at the time of the search, police officers who permitted members of the media to accompany them were entitled to qualified immunity as defendants in a lawsuit under 42 U.S.C. § 1983, charging them with a violation of the rights of the persons whose home was searched. Id. (8–1).

United States v. Stefonek, 179 F.3d 1030 (7th Cir.1999) (particularity requirement not met; but since no interest of defendant was violated, suppression not ordered).

Page 218

Rule 41(c)(1). See Appendix.

Page 220

Rule 41(d). See Appendix.

Page 229

114. In United States v. Myers, 308 F.3d 251 (3d Cir.2002), the court considered at length the permissible scope of a search incident to an arrest. Distinguishing the search of the passenger compartment of an automobile after the driver's arrest, which is governed by the *Belton* rule (Casebook, p. 231, Note 117), the court said that a search incident to an arrest is "reasonable" under the Fourth Amendment only "when it is confined to, and controlled by, the circumstances that warrant the intrusion," 308 F.3d at 266. Noting that the defendant, who was handcuffed behind his back, lying face down, and watched by two armed police officers, would have to have been an acrobat or a Houdini to gain access to a school bag lying a few feet from him, the court held that a search of the bag by a third police officer was not permissible.

Page 232

117. United States v. McLaughlin, 170 F.3d 889 (9th Cir.1999) (search of car five minutes after driver had been removed from scene was "incident to arrest").

Page 245

Illinois v. McArthur

531 U.S. 326, 121 S.Ct. 946, 148 L.Ed.2d 838 (2001).

■ JUSTICE BREYER delivered the opinion of the Court.

Police officers, with probable cause to believe that a man had hidden marijuana in his home, prevented that man from entering the home for about two hours while they obtained a search warrant. We must decide whether those officers violated the Fourth Amendment. We conclude that the officers acted reasonably. They did not violate the Amendment's requirements. And we reverse an Illinois court's holding to the contrary.

I

A

On April 2, 1997, Tera McArthur asked two police officers to accompany her to the trailer where she lived with her husband, Charles, so that they could keep the peace while she removed her belongings. The two officers, Assistant Chief John Love and Officer Richard Skidis, arrived with Tera at the trailer at about 3:15 p.m. Tera went inside, where Charles was present. The officers remained outside.

When Tera emerged after collecting her possessions, she spoke to Chief Love, who was then on the porch. She suggested he check the trailer because "Chuck had dope in there." App. 15. She added (in Love's words) that she had seen Chuck "slid[e] some dope underneath the couch." Id. at 19.

Love knocked on the trailer door, told Charles what Tera had said, and asked for permission to search the trailer, which Charles denied. Love then sent Officer Skidis with Tera to get a search warrant.

Love told Charles, who by this time was also on the porch, that he could not reenter the trailer unless a police officer accompanied him. Charles subsequently reentered the trailer two or three times (to get cigarettes and to make phone calls), and each time Love stood just inside the door to observe what Charles did.

Officer Skidis obtained the warrant by about 5 p.m. He returned to the trailer and, along with other officers, searched it. The officers found under the sofa a marijuana pipe, a box for marijuana (called a "one-hitter" box), and a small amount of marijuana. They then arrested Charles.

B

Illinois subsequently charged Charles McArthur with unlawfully possessing drug paraphernalia and marijuana (less than 2.5 grams), both misdemeanors. . . . McArthur moved to suppress the pipe, box, and marijuana on the ground that they were the "fruit" of an unlawful police seizure, namely, the refusal to let him reenter the trailer unaccompanied, which would have permitted him, he said, to "have destroyed the marijuana." App. 27.

The trial court granted McArthur's suppression motion. The Appellate court of Illinois affirmed ... and the Illinois Supreme court denied the State's petition for leave to appeal.... We granted certiorari to determine whether the Fourth Amendment prohibits the kind of temporary seizure at issue here.

II

A

The Fourth Amendment says that the "right of the people to be secure in their persons, houses, papers, and effects, against unreasonable searches and seizures, shall not be violated." U.S. Const., Amdt 4. Its "central requirement" is one of reasonableness. See Texas v. Brown, 460 U.S. 730, 739 (1983). In order to enforce that requirement, this Court has interpreted the Amendment as establishing rules and presumptions designed to control conduct of law enforcement officers that may significantly intrude upon privacy interests. Sometimes those rules require warrants. We have said, for example, that in "the ordinary case," seizures of personal property are "unreasonable within the meaning of the Fourth Amendment," without more, "unless ... accomplished pursuant to a judicial warrant," issued by a neutral magistrate after finding probable cause. United States v. Place, 462 U.S. 696, 701 (1983).

We nonetheless have made it clear that there are exceptions to the warrant requirement. When faced with special law enforcement needs, diminished expectations of privacy, minimal intrusions, or the like, the Court has found that certain general, or individual, circumstances may render a warrantless search or seizure reasonable....

In the circumstances of the case before us, we cannot say that the warrantless seizure was *per se* unreasonable. It involves a plausible claim of specially pressing or urgent law enforcement need, i.e., "exigent circumstances." ... Moreover, the restraint at issue was tailored to that need, being limited in time and scope ... and avoiding significant intrusion into the home itself.... Consequently, rather than employing a *per se* rule of unreasonableness, we balance the privacy-related and law enforcement-related concerns to determine if the intrusion was reasonable....

We conclude that the restriction at issue was reasonable, and hence lawful, in light of the following circumstances, which we consider in combination. First, the police had probable cause to believe that McArthur's trailer home contained evidence of a crime and contraband, namely, unlawful drugs. The police had had an opportunity to speak with Tera McArthur and make at least a rough assessment of her reliability. They knew she had had a firsthand opportunity to observe her husband's behavior, in particular with respect to the drugs at issue. And they thought, with good reason, that her report to them reflected that opportunity. . . .

Second, the police had good reason to fear that, unless restrained, McArthur would destroy the drugs before they could return with a warrant. They reasonably might have thought that McArthur realized that his wife knew about his marijuana stash; observed that she was angry or frightened enough to ask the police to accompany her; saw that after leaving the trailer she had spoken with the police; and noticed that she had walked off with one policeman while leaving the other outside to observe the trailer. They reasonably could have concluded that McArthur, consequently suspecting an imminent search, would, if given the chance, get rid of the drugs fast.

Third, the police made reasonable efforts to reconcile their law enforcement needs with the demands of personal privacy. They neither searched the trailer nor arrested McArthur before obtaining a warrant. Rather, they imposed a significantly less restrictive restraint, preventing McArthur only from entering the trailer unaccompanied. They left his home and his belongings intact—until a neutral Magistrate, finding probable cause, issued a warrant.

Fourth, the police imposed the restraint for a limited period of time, namely, two hours. . . . As far as the record reveals, this time period was no longer than reasonably necessary for the police, acting with diligence, to obtain the warrant. . . . Given the nature of the intrusion and the law enforcement interest at stake, this brief seizure of the premises was permissible.

B

. . .

In various other circumstances, this Court has upheld temporary restraints where needed to preserve evidence until police could obtain a warrant. . . .

We have found no case in which this Court has held unlawful a temporary seizure that was supported by probable cause and was designed to prevent the loss of evidence while the police diligently obtained a warrant in a reasonable period of time. . . .

C

Nor are we persuaded by the countervailing considerations that the parties or lower courts have raised. McArthur argues that the police proceeded without probable cause. But McArthur has waived this argument. . . . And in any event, it is without merit. . . .

The Appellate Court of Illinois concluded that the police could not order McArthur to stay outside his home because McArthur's porch, where he stood at the time, was part of his home; hence the order "amounted to a constructive eviction" of McArthur from his residence. 713 N.E.2d [93 (1999)], at 98. This Court has held, however, that a person standing in the doorway of a house is "in a 'public' place," and hence subject to arrest without a warrant permitting entry of the home.... Regardless, we do not believe the difference to which the Appellate Court points—porch versus, e.g., front walk—could make a significant difference as to the reasonableness of the police restraint; and that, from the Fourth Amendment's perspective, is what matters.

The Appellate Court also found negatively significant the fact that Chief Love, with McArthur's consent, stepped inside the trailer's doorway to observe McArthur when McArthur reentered the trailer on two or three occasions.... McArthur, however, reentered simply for his own convenience, to make phone calls and to obtain cigarettes. Under these circumstances, the reasonableness of the greater restriction (preventing reentry) implies the reasonableness of the lesser (permitting reentry conditioned on observation).

Finally, McArthur points to a case (and we believe it is the only case) that he believes offers direct support, namely, Welsh v. Wisconsin, [466 U.S. 740 (1984)]. In *Welsh*, this Court held that police could not enter a home without a warrant in order to prevent the loss of evidence (namely, the defendant's blood alcohol level) of the "nonjailable traffic offense" of driving while intoxicated. 466 U.S. at 742, 754. McArthur notes that his two convictions are for misdemeanors, which, he says, are as minor, and he adds that the restraint, keeping him out of his home, was nearly as serious.

We nonetheless find significant distinctions. The evidence at issue here was of crimes that were "jailable," not "nonjailable." ... In *Welsh*, we noted that, "[g]iven that the classification of state crimes differs widely among the States, the penalty that may attach to any particular offense seems to provide the clearest and most consistent indication of the State's interest in arresting individuals suspected of committing that offense." 466 U.S., at 754, n.14. The same reasoning applies here, where class C misdemeanors include such widely diverse offenses as drag racing, drinking alcohol in a railroad car or on a railroad platform, bribery by a candidate for public office, and assault....

And the restriction at issue here is less serious. Temporarily keeping a person from entering his home, a consequence whenever police stop a person on the street, is considerably less intrusive than police entry into the home itself in order to make a warrantless arrest or conduct a search....

We have explained above why we believe that the need to preserve evidence of a "jailable" offense was sufficiently urgent or pressing to justify the restriction upon entry that the police imposed. We need not decide whether the circumstances before us would have justified a greater restriction for this type of offense or the same restriction were only a "nonjailable" offense at issue.

III

In sum, the police officers in this case had probable cause to believe that a home contained contraband, which was evidence of a crime. They reasonably believed that the home's resident, if left free of any restraint, would destroy that evidence. And they imposed a restraint that was both limited and tailored reasonably to secure law enforcement needs while protecting privacy interests. In our view, the restraint met the Fourth Amendment's demands.

. . . [*]

Page 252

123. In Maryland v. Dyson, 527 U.S. 465 (1999) (per curiam), the Court emphasized again that if there is a probable cause to search a car, a warrant need not be obtained, even if there is time to do so.

Page 253

Wyoming v. Houghton

526 U.S. 295, 119 S.Ct. 1297, 143 L.Ed.2d 408 (1999).

■ JUSTICE SCALIA delivered the opinion of the Court.

This case presents the question whether police officers violate the Fourth Amendment when they search a passenger's personal belongings inside an automobile that they have probable cause to believe contains contraband.

I

In the early morning hours of July 23, 1995, a Wyoming Highway Patrol officer stopped an automobile for speeding and driving with a faulty brake light. There were three passengers in the front seat of the car: David Young (the driver), his girlfriend, and respondent. While questioning Young, the officer noticed a hypodermic syringe in Young's shirt pocket. He left the occupants under the supervision of two backup officers as he went to get gloves from his patrol car. Upon his return, he instructed Young to step out of the car and place the syringe on the hood. The officer then

[*] Justice Souter wrote a concurring opinion. Justice Stevens wrote a dissenting opinion.

asked Young why he had a syringe; with refreshing candor, Young replied that he used it to take drugs.

At this point, the backup officers ordered the two female passengers out of the car and asked them for identification. Respondent falsely identified herself as "Sandra James" and stated that she did not have any identification. Meanwhile, in light of Young's admission, the officer searched the passenger compartment of the car for contraband. On the back seat, he found a purse, which respondent claimed as hers. He removed from the purse a wallet containing respondent's driver's license, identifying her properly as Sandra K. Houghton. When the officer asked her why she had lied about her name, she replied: "In case things went bad."

Continuing his search of the purse, the officer found a brown pouch and a black wallet-type container. Respondent denied that the former was hers, and claimed ignorance of how it came to be there; it was found to contain drug paraphernalia and a syringe with 60 ccs of methamphetamine. Respondent admitted ownership of the black container, which was also found to contain drug paraphernalia, and a syringe (which respondent acknowledged was hers) with 10 ccs of methamphetamine—an amount insufficient to support the felony conviction at issue in this case. The officer also found fresh needle-track marks on respondent's arms. He placed her under arrest.

The State of Wyoming charged respondent with felony possession of methamphetamine in a liquid amount greater than three-tenths of a gram. . . . After a hearing, the trial court denied her motion to suppress all evidence obtained from the purse as the fruit of a violation of the Fourth and Fourteenth Amendments. The court held that the officer had probable cause to search the car for contraband, and, by extension, any containers therein that could hold such contraband. A jury convicted respondent as charged.

The Wyoming Supreme Court, by divided vote, reversed the conviction and announced the following rule:

> "Generally, once probable cause is established to search a vehicle, an officer is entitled to search all containers therein which may contain the object of the search. However, if the officer knows or should know that a container is the personal effect of a passenger who is not suspected of criminal activity, then the container is outside the scope of the search unless someone had the opportunity to conceal the contraband within the personal effect to avoid detection." 956 P.2d 363, 372 (1998).

The court held that the search of respondent's purse violated the Fourth and Fourteenth Amendments because the officer "knew or should have known that the purse did not belong to the driver, but to one of the passengers," and because "there was no probable cause to search the passengers' personal effects and no reason to believe that contraband had been placed within the purse." Ibid.

II

The Fourth Amendment protects "[t]he right of the people to be secure in their persons, houses, papers, and effects, against unreasonable searches and seizures." In determining whether a particular governmental action violates this provision, we inquire first whether the action was regarded as an unlawful search or seizure under the common law when the Amendment was framed.... Where that inquiry yields no answer, we must evaluate the search or seizure under traditional standards of reasonableness by assessing, on the one hand, the degree to which it intrudes upon an individual's privacy and, on the other, the degree to which it is needed for the promotion of legitimate governmental interests....

It is uncontested in the present case that the police officers had probable cause to believe there were illegal drugs in the car. Carroll v. United States, 267 U.S. 132 (1925), similarly involved the warrantless search of a car that law enforcement officials had probable cause to believe contained contraband—in that case, bootleg liquor. The Court concluded that the Framers would have regarded such a search as reasonable in light of legislation enacted by Congress from 1789 through 1799—as well as subsequent legislation from the Founding era and beyond—that empowered customs officials to search any ship or vessel without a warrant if they had probable cause to believe that it contained goods subject to a duty. Id., at 150–153. Thus, the Court held that "contraband goods concealed and illegally transported in an automobile or other vehicle may be searched for without a warrant" where probable cause exists. *Carroll*, supra, at 153.

We have furthermore read the historical evidence to show that the Framers would have regarded as reasonable (if there was probable cause) the warrantless search of containers *within* an automobile. In [United States v.] *Ross*, [456 U.S. 798 (1982)], we upheld as reasonable the warrantless search of a paper bag and leather pouch found in the trunk of the defendant's car by officers who had probable cause to believe that the trunk contained drugs....

Ross summarized its holding as follows: "If probable cause justifies the search of a lawfully stopped vehicle, it justifies the search of *every part of the vehicle and its contents* that may conceal the object of the search." Id., at 825 (emphasis added). And our later cases describing *Ross* have characterized it as applying broadly to *all* containers within a car, without qualification as to ownership....

To be sure, there was no passenger in *Ross*, and it was not claimed that the package in the trunk belonged to anyone other than the driver. Even so, if the rule of law that *Ross* announced were limited to contents belonging to the driver, or contents other than those belonging to passengers, one would have expected that substantial limitation to be expressed.

And, more importantly, one would have expected that limitation to be apparent in the historical evidence that formed the basis for *Ross*'s holding. In fact, however, nothing in the statutes *Ross* relied upon, or in the practice under those statutes, would except from authorized warrantless search packages belonging to passengers on the suspect ship, horse-drawn carriage, or automobile.

Finally, we must observe that the analytical principle underlying the rule announced in *Ross* is fully consistent—as respondent's proposal is not—with the balance of our Fourth Amendment jurisprudence. *Ross* concluded from the historical evidence that the permissible scope of a warrantless car search "is defined by the object of the search and the places in which there is probable cause to believe that it may be found." 456 U.S., at 824. . . .

In sum, neither *Ross* itself nor the historical evidence it relied upon admits of a distinction among packages or containers based on ownership. When there is probable cause to search for contraband in a car, it is reasonable for police officers—like customs officials in the Founding era—to examine packages and containers without a showing of individualized probable cause for each one. A passenger's personal belongings, just like the driver's belongings or containers attached to the car like a glove compartment, are "in" the car, and the officer has probable cause to search for contraband in the car.

Even if the historical evidence, as described by Ross, were thought to be equivocal, we would find that the balancing of the relative interests weighs decidedly in favor of allowing searches of a passenger's belongings. Passengers, no less than drivers, possess a reduced expectation of privacy with regard to the property that they transport in cars, which "trave[l] public thoroughfares," Cardwell v. Lewis, 417 U.S. 583, 590 (1974), "seldom serv[e] as . . . the repository of personal effects," ibid., are subjected to police stop and examination to enforce "pervasive" governmental controls "[a]s an everyday occurrence," South Dakota v. Opperman, 428 U.S. 364, 368 (1976), and, finally, are exposed to traffic accidents that may render all their contents open to public scrutiny.

. . .

Whereas the passenger's privacy expectations are, as we have described, considerably diminished, the governmental interests at stake are substantial. Effective law enforcement would be appreciably impaired without the ability to search a passenger's personal belongings when there is reason to believe contraband or evidence of criminal wrongdoing is hidden in the car. As in all car-search cases, the "ready mobility" of an automobile creates a risk that the evidence or contraband will be permanently lost while a warrant is obtained. . . . In addition, a car passenger . . . will often be engaged in a common enterprise with the driver, and have the same interest in concealing the fruits or the evidence of their wrongdoing. . . . A criminal might be able to hide contraband in a passenger's belongings as readily as in other containers in the car . . . perhaps even surreptitiously, without the passenger's knowledge or permission. (This last possibility provided the basis for respondent's defense at trial; she testified that most of the seized contraband must have been placed in her purse by her traveling companions at one or another of various times, including the time she was "half asleep" in the car.)

To be sure, these factors favoring a search will not always be present, but the balancing of interests must be conducted with an eye to the generality of cases. To require that the investigating officer have positive reason to believe that the passenger and driver were engaged in a common enterprise, or positive reason to believe that the driver had time and occasion to conceal the item in the passenger's belongings, surreptitiously or with friendly permission, is to impose requirements so seldom met that a "passenger's property" rule would dramatically reduce the ability to find and seize contraband and evidence of crime. Of course these requirements would not attach (under the Wyoming Supreme Court's rule) until the police officer knows or has reason to know that the container belongs to a passenger. But once a "passenger's property" exception to car searches became widely known, one would expect passenger-confederates to claim everything as their own. And one would anticipate a bog of litigation—in the form of both civil lawsuits and motions to suppress in criminal trials—involving such questions as whether the officer should have believed a passenger's claim of ownership, whether he should have inferred ownership from various objective factors, whether he had probable cause to believe that the passenger was a confederate, or to believe that the driver might have introduced the contraband into the package with or without the passenger's knowledge. When balancing the competing interests, our determinations of "reasonableness" under the Fourth Amendment must take account of these practical realities. We think they militate in favor of the needs of law enforcement, and against a personal-privacy interest that is ordinarily weak.

Finally, if we were to invent an exception from the historical practice that *Ross* accurately described and summarized, it is perplexing why that exception should protect only property belonging to a passenger, rather than (what seems much more logical) property belonging to anyone other than the driver. Surely Houghton's privacy would have been invaded to the same degree whether she was present or absent when her purse was searched. And surely her presence in the car with the driver provided more, rather than less, reason to believe that the two were in league. It may ordinarily be easier to identify the property as belonging to someone other than the driver when the purported owner is present to identify it—but in the many cases (like *Ross* itself) where the car is seized, that identification may occur later, at the station-house; and even at the site of the stop one can readily imagine a package clearly marked with the owner's name and phone number, by which the officer can confirm the driver's denial of ownership. The sensible rule (and the one supported by history and caselaw) is that such a package may be searched, whether or not its owner is present as a passenger or otherwise, because it may contain the contraband that the officer has reason to believe is in the car.

. . .

We hold that police officers with probable cause to search a car may inspect passengers' belongings found in the car that are capable of concealing the object of the search. The judgment of the Wyoming Supreme Court is reversed.[*]

Page 254

Knowles v. Iowa

525 U.S. 113, 119 S.Ct. 484, 142 L.Ed.2d 492 (1998).

■ CHIEF JUSTICE REHNQUIST delivered the opinion of the Court.

An Iowa police officer stopped petitioner Knowles for speeding, but issued him a citation rather than arresting him. The question presented is whether such a procedure authorizes the officer, consistently with the Fourth Amendment, to conduct a full search of the car. We answer this question "no."

Knowles was stopped in Newton, Iowa, after having been clocked driving 43 miles per hour on a road where the speed limit was 25 miles per hour. The police officer issued a citation to Knowles, although under Iowa law he might have arrested him. The officer then conducted a full search of the car, and under the driver's seat he found a bag of marijuana and a "pot pipe." Knowles was then arrested and charged with violation of state laws dealing with controlled substances.

Before trial, Knowles moved to suppress the evidence so obtained. He argued that the search could not be sustained under the "search incident to arrest" exception recognized in United States v. Robinson, 414 U.S. 218 (1973), because he had not been placed under arrest. At the hearing on the motion to suppress, the police officer conceded that he had neither Knowles' consent nor probable cause to conduct the search. He relied on Iowa law dealing with such searches.

Iowa Code Ann. § 321.485(1)(a) (West 1997) provides that Iowa peace officers having cause to believe that a person has violated any traffic or motor vehicle equipment law may arrest the person and immediately take the person before a magistrate. Iowa law also authorizes the far more usual practice of issuing a citation in lieu of arrest or in lieu of continued custody

[*] Justice Breyer wrote a concurring opinion. Justice Stevens wrote a dissenting opinion, which Justice Souter and Justice Ginsburg joined.

after an initial arrest.... Section 805.1(4) provides that the issuance of a citation in lieu of an arrest "does not affect the officer's authority to conduct an otherwise lawful search." The Iowa Supreme Court has interpreted this provision as providing authority to officers to conduct a full-blown search of an automobile and driver in those cases where police elect not to make a custodial arrest and instead issue a citation—that is, a search incident to citation....

Based on this authority, the trial court denied the motion to suppress and found Knowles guilty. The Supreme Court of Iowa, sitting en banc, affirmed by a divided vote.... We granted certiorari ... and we now reverse.

. . .

In *Robinson*, supra, we noted the two historical rationales for the "search incident to arrest" exception: (1) the need to disarm the suspect in order to take him into custody, and (2) the need to preserve evidence for later use at trial.... But neither of these underlying rationales for the search incident to arrest exception is sufficient to justify the search in the present case.

We have recognized that the first rationale—officer safety—is " 'both legitimate and weighty,' " Maryland v. Wilson, 519 U.S. 408, 412 (1997) (quoting Pennsylvania v. Mimms, 434 U.S. 106, 110 (1977) (per curiam)). The threat to officer safety from issuing a traffic citation, however, is a good deal less than in the case of a custodial arrest. In *Robinson*, we stated that a custodial arrest involves "danger to an officer" because of "the extended exposure which follows the taking of a suspect into custody and transporting him to the police station." 414 U.S., at 234–235. We recognized that "[t]he danger to the police officer flows from the fact of the arrest, and its attendant proximity, stress, and uncertainty, and not from the grounds for arrest." Id., at 234, n.5. A routine traffic stop, on the other hand, is a relatively brief encounter and "is more analogous to a so-called '*Terry* stop' ... than to a formal arrest." Berkemer v. McCarty, 468 U.S. 420, 437 (1984)....

This is not to say that the concern for officer safety is absent in the case of a routine traffic stop. It plainly is not.... But while the concern for officer safety in this context may justify the "minimal" additional intrusion of ordering a driver and passengers out of the car, it does not by itself justify the often considerably greater intrusion attending a full field-type search. Even without the search authority Iowa urges, officers have other, independent bases to search for weapons and protect themselves from danger. For example, they may order out of a vehicle both the driver ... and any passengers ...; perform a "patdown" of a driver and any passengers upon reasonable suspicion that they may be armed and dangerous ...; conduct a "*Terry* patdown" of the passenger compartment of a vehicle upon reasonable suspicion that an occupant is dangerous and may gain immediate control of a weapon ...; and even conduct a full search of the passenger compartment, including any containers therein, pursuant to a custodial arrest....

Nor has Iowa shown the second justification for the authority to search incident to arrest—the need to discover and preserve evidence. Once Knowles was stopped for speeding and issued a citation, all the evidence necessary to prosecute that offense had been obtained. No further evidence of excessive speed was going to be found either on the person of the offender or in the passenger compartment of the car.

Iowa nevertheless argues that a "search incident to citation" is justified because a suspect who is subject to a routine traffic stop may attempt to hide or destroy evidence related to his identity (e.g., a driver's license or vehicle registration), or destroy evidence of another, as yet undetected crime. As for the destruction of evidence relating to identity, if a police officer is not satisfied with the identification furnished by the driver, this may be a basis for arresting him rather than merely issuing a citation. As for destroying evidence of other crimes, the possibility that an officer would stumble onto evidence wholly unrelated to the speeding offense seems remote.

In *Robinson*, we held that the authority to conduct a full field search as incident to an arrest was a "bright-line rule," which was based on the concern for officer safety and destruction or loss of evidence, but which did not depend in every case upon the existence of either concern. Here we are asked to extend that "bright-line rule" to a situation where the concern for officer safety is not present to the same extent and the concern for destruction or loss of evidence is not present at all. We decline to do so. The judgment of the Supreme Court of Iowa is reversed, and the cause remanded for further proceedings not inconsistent with this opinion.

It is so ordered.

Page 263

133. The ruling in *Mincey* that there is no general crime-scene exception to the requirement of a warrant is confirmed in Flippo v. West Virginia, 528 U.S. 11 (1999) (per curiam).

Ingram v. City of Columbus, 185 F.3d 579 (6th Cir.1999) (officers entering premises pursuant to exigent circumstances do not have general authority to handcuff occupants and detain them at gunpoint).

Page 264

See United States v. Simons, 206 F.3d 392 (4th Cir.2000) (employer's viewing of defendant's computer files and entry into defendant's office to retrieve his hard drive upheld).

Page 275

The warrantless seizure from a public place of a car that the police have probable cause to believe is forfeitable contraband is not a violation of the Fourth Amendment. Florida v. White, 526 U.S. 559 (1999) (7–2). The car was subject to forfeiture under a state statute because it had been used in drug transactions.

140. See United States v. Runyan, 275 F.3d 449 (5th Cir.2001), appeal after remand, 290 F.3d 223 (2002), discussing the permissible scope of a warrantless police search following a private search, reported to the police, of the same premises or containers.

Page 288

143. A patient in a state psychiatric hospital has a reasonable expectation of privacy in the portion of a shared room occupied by him. State v. Stott, 794 A.2d 120 (N.J.2002).

Page 289

In United States v. Twilley, 222 F.3d 1092 (9th Cir.2000), the court said that although the defendant, as a passenger in a car, had no standing to challenge the search of the car, he had standing to challenge the initial stop. Furthermore, because the initial stop violated the Fourth Amendment, the items seized would be suppressed as fruit of the poisonous tree.

Page 290

United States v. Gamez-Orduño, 235 F.3d 453 (9th Cir.2000). Defendants, who were smuggling drugs, stayed overnight in a trailer at the invitation of the occupant. The court held that, notwithstanding their illegal business, they were overnight guests and, under Minnesota v. Olson (Casebook, p. 283), had standing to contest the search of the trailer.

Minnesota v. Carter

525 U.S. 83, 119 S.Ct. 469, 142 L.Ed.2d 373 (1998).

■ CHIEF JUSTICE REHNQUIST delivered the opinion of the Court.

Respondents and the lessee of an apartment were sitting in one of its rooms, bagging cocaine. While so engaged they were observed by a police officer, who looked through a drawn window blind. The Supreme Court of Minnesota held that the officer's viewing was a search which violated respondents' Fourth Amendment rights. We hold that no such violation occurred.

James Thielen, a police officer in the Twin Cities' suburb of Eagan, Minnesota, went to an apartment building to investigate a tip from a confidential informant. The informant said that he had walked by the window of a ground-floor apartment and had seen people putting a white powder into bags. The officer looked in the same window through a gap in the closed blind and observed the bagging operation for several minutes. He then notified headquarters, which began preparing affidavits for a search warrant while he returned to the apartment building. When two men left the building in a previously identified Cadillac, the police stopped the car. Inside were respondents Carter and Johns. As the police opened the door of the car to let Johns out, they observed a black zippered pouch and a handgun, later determined to be loaded, on the vehicle's floor. Carter and Johns were arrested, and a later police search of the vehicle the next day discovered pagers, a scale, and 47 grams of cocaine in plastic sandwich bags.

After seizing the car, the police returned to Apartment 103 and arrested the occupant, Kimberly Thompson, who is not a party to this appeal. A search of the apartment pursuant to a warrant revealed cocaine residue on the kitchen table and plastic baggies similar to those found in the Cadillac. Thielen identified Carter, Johns, and Thompson as the three people he had observed placing the powder into baggies. The police later learned that while Thompson was the lessee of the apartment, Carter and Johns lived in Chicago and had come to the apartment for the sole purpose of packaging the cocaine. Carter and Johns had never been to the apartment before and were only in the apartment for approximately 2½ hours. In return for the use of the apartment, Carter and Johns had given Thompson one-eighth of an ounce of the cocaine.

Carter and Johns were charged with conspiracy to commit controlled substance crime in the first degree and aiding and abetting in a controlled substance crime in the first degree.... They moved to suppress all evidence obtained from the apartment and the Cadillac, as well as to suppress several post-arrest incriminating statements they had made. They argued that Thielen's initial observation of their drug packaging activities was an unreasonable search in violation of the Fourth Amendment and that all evidence obtained as a result of this unreasonable search was inadmissible as fruit of the poisonous tree. The Minnesota trial court held that since, unlike the defendant in Minnesota v. Olson, 495 U.S. 91 (1990), Carter and Johns were not overnight social guests but temporary out-of-state visitors, they were not entitled to claim the protection of the Fourth Amendment against the government intrusion into the apartment. The trial court also concluded that Thielen's observation was not a search within the meaning of the Fourth Amendment. After a trial, Carter and Johns were each convicted of both offenses....

A divided Minnesota Supreme Court reversed, holding that respondents had "standing" to claim the protection of the Fourth Amendment because they had " 'a legitimate expectation of privacy in the invaded place.' " 569 N.W. 2d 169, 174 (1997) (quoting Rakas v. Illinois, 439 U.S. 128, 143 (1978)). The court noted that even though "society does not recognize as valuable the task of bagging cocaine, we conclude that society does recognize as valuable the right of property owners or leaseholders to invite persons into the privacy of their homes to conduct a common task, be it legal or illegal activity. We, therefore, hold that [respondents] had standing to bring [their] motion to suppress the evidence gathered as a result of Thielen's observations." 569 N.W. 2d, at 176.... Based upon its conclusion that the respondents had "standing" to raise their Fourth Amendment claims, the court went on to hold that Thielen's observation constituted a search of the apartment under the Fourth Amendment, and that the search was unreasonable. Id., at 176–179. We granted certiorari ... and now reverse.

The Minnesota courts analyzed whether respondents had a legitimate expectation of privacy under the rubric of "standing" doctrine, an analysis which this Court expressly rejected 20 years ago in *Rakas*. 439 U.S., at 139–140. In that case, we held that automobile passengers could not assert the protection of the Fourth Amendment against the seizure of incriminating evidence from a vehicle where they owned neither the vehicle nor the evidence. Ibid. Central to our analysis was the idea that in determining whether a defendant is able to show the violation of his (and not someone else's) Fourth Amendment rights, the "definition of those rights is more properly placed within the purview of substantive Fourth Amendment law than within that of standing." 439 U.S., at 140. Thus, we held that in order to claim the protection of the Fourth Amendment, a defendant must demonstrate that he personally has an expectation of privacy in the place searched, and that his expectation is reasonable; i.e., one which has "a source outside of the Fourth Amendment, either by reference to concepts of real or personal property law or to understandings that are recognized and permitted by society." Id., at 143–144, and n.12....

The Fourth Amendment ... protects persons against unreasonable searches of "their persons [and] houses" and thus indicates that the Fourth Amendment is a personal right that must be invoked by an individual. See Katz v. United States, 389 U.S. 347, 351 (1967) ("[T]he Fourth Amendment protects people, not places"). But the extent to which the Fourth Amendment protects people may depend upon where those people are. We have held that "capacity to claim the protection of the Fourth Amendment depends ... upon whether the person who claims the protection of the Amendment has a legitimate expectation of privacy in the invaded place." *Rakas*, supra, at 143....

The text of the Amendment suggests that its protections extend only to people in "their" houses. But we have held that in some circumstances a person may have a legitimate expectation of privacy in the house of someone else. In Minnesota v. Olson, 495 U.S. 91 (1990), for example, we decided that an overnight guest in a house had the sort of expectation of privacy that the Fourth Amendment protects....

... Thus an overnight guest in a home may claim the protection of the Fourth Amendment, but one who is merely present with the consent of the householder may not.

Respondents here were obviously not overnight guests, but were essentially present for a business transaction and were only in the home a matter of hours. There is no suggestion that they had a previous relationship with Thompson, or that there was any other purpose to their visit. Nor was there anything similar to the overnight guest relationship in *Olson* to suggest a degree of acceptance into the household. While the apartment was a dwelling place for Thompson, it was for these respondents simply a place to do business.

Property used for commercial purposes is treated differently for Fourth Amendment purposes than residential property. "An expectation of privacy in commercial premises, however, is different from, and indeed less than, a similar expectation in an individual's home." New York v. Burger, 482 U.S. 691, 700 (1987). And while it was a "home" in which respondents were present, it was not their home. Similarly, the Court has held that in some circumstances a worker can claim Fourth Amendment protection over his own workplace. See, e.g., O'Connor v. Ortega, 480 U.S. 709 (1987). But there is no indication that respondents in this case had nearly as significant a connection to Thompson's apartment as the worker in *O'Connor* had to his own private office. See id., at 716–17.

If we regard the overnight guest in Minnesota v. Olson as typifying those who may claim the protection of the Fourth Amendment in the home of another, and one merely "legitimately on the premises" as typifying those who may not do so, the present case is obviously somewhere in between. But the purely commercial nature of the transaction engaged in here, the relatively short period of time on the premises, and the lack of any previous connection between respondents and the householder, all lead us to conclude that respondents' situation is closer to that of one simply permitted on the premises. We therefore hold that any search which may have occurred did not violate their Fourth Amendment rights.

Because we conclude that respondents had no legitimate expectation of privacy in the apartment, we need not decide whether the police officer's observation constituted a "search." The judgment of the Supreme Court of Minnesota is accordingly reversed, and the cause is remanded for proceedings not inconsistent with this opinion.

■ JUSTICE SCALIA, with whom JUSTICE THOMAS joins, concurring.

I join the opinion of the Court because I believe it accurately applies our recent case law, including Minnesota v. Olson, 495 U.S. 91 (1990). I write separately to express my view that that case law—like the submissions of the parties in this case—gives short shrift to the text of the Fourth Amendment, and to the well and long understood meaning of that text. Specifically, it leaps to apply the fuzzy standard of "legitimate expectation of privacy"—a consideration that is often relevant to whether a search or seizure covered by the Fourth Amendment is "unreasonable"—to the threshold question whether a search or seizure covered by the Fourth Amendment *has occurred*. If that latter question is addressed first and analyzed under the text of the Constitution as traditionally understood, the present case is not remotely difficult.

The Fourth Amendment protects "[t]he right of the people to be secure in *their* persons, houses, papers, and effects, against unreasonable searches and seizures ...." U.S. Const., Amdt. 4 (emphasis added). It must be acknowledged that the phrase "their ... houses" in this provision is, in isolation, ambiguous. It could mean "their respective houses," so that the protection extends to each person only in his own house. But it could also mean "their respective and each other's houses," so that each person would be protected even when visiting the house of someone else. As today's opinion for the Court suggests, however, ante, at 88–90, it is not linguistically possible to give the provision the latter, expansive interpretation with respect to "houses" without giving it the same interpretation with respect to the nouns that are parallel to "houses"—"persons, ... papers, and effects"—which would give me a constitutional right not to have your person unreasonably searched. This is so absurd that it has to my knowledge never been contemplated. The obvious meaning of the provision is that *each* person has the right to be secure against unreasonable searches and seizures in *his own* person, house, papers, and effects.

The Founding-era materials that I have examined confirm that this was the understood meaning....

. . .

Of course this is not to say that the Fourth Amendment protects only the Lord of the Manor who holds his estate in fee simple. People call a house "their" home when legal title is in the bank, when they rent it, and even when they merely occupy it rent-free—*so long as they actually live there.* ...

...[I]n deciding the question presented today we write upon a slate that is far from clean.... We went to the absolute limit of what text and tradition permit in Minnesota v. Olson, 495 U.S. 91 (1990), when we protected a mere overnight guest against an unreasonable search of his hosts' apartment. But whereas it is plausible to regard a person's overnight lodging as at least his "temporary" residence, it is entirely impossible to give that characterization to an apartment that he uses to package cocaine. Respondents here were not searched in "their ... hous[e]" under any interpretation of the phrase that bears the remotest relationship to the well understood meaning of the Fourth Amendment.

. . .

■ JUSTICE KENNEDY, concurring.

I join the Court's opinion, for its reasoning is consistent with my view that almost all social guests have a legitimate expectation of privacy, and hence protection against unreasonable searches, in their host's home.

. . .

The homeowner's right to privacy is not at issue in this case. The Court does not reach the question whether the officer's unaided observations of Thompson's apartment constituted a search. If there was in fact a search, however, then Thompson had the right to object to the unlawful police surveillance of her apartment and the right to suppress any evidence disclosed by the search. Similarly, if the police had entered her home without a search warrant to arrest respondents, Thompson's own privacy interests would be violated and she could presumably bring an action under 42 U.S.C. § 1983 or an action for trespass. Our cases establish, however, that respondents have no independent privacy right, the violation of which results in exclusion of evidence against them, unless they can establish a meaningful connection to Thompson's apartment.

The settled rule is that the requisite connection is an expectation of privacy that society recognizes as reasonable. Katz v. United States, 389 U.S. 347, 361 (1967) (Harlan, J., concurring). The application of that rule involves consideration of the kind of place in which the individual claims the privacy interest and what expectations of privacy are traditional and well recognized. Ibid. I would expect that most, if not all, social guests legitimately expect that, in accordance with social custom, the homeowner will exercise her discretion to include or exclude others for the guests' benefit. As we recognized in Minnesota v. Olson, 495 U.S. 91 (1990), where these social expectations exist—as in the case of an overnight guest—they are sufficient to create a legitimate expectation of privacy, even in the absence of any property right to exclude others. In this respect, the dissent must be correct that reasonable expectations of the owner are shared, to some extent, by the guest. This analysis suggests that, as a general rule, social guests will have an expectation of privacy in their host's home. That is not the case before us, however.

In this case respondents have established nothing more than a fleeting and insubstantial connection with Thompson's home. For all that appears in the record, respondents used Thompson's house simply as a convenient processing station, their purpose involving nothing more than the mechanical act of chopping and packing a substance for distribution. There is no suggestion that respondents engaged in confidential communications with Thompson about their transaction. Respondents had not been to Thompson's apartment before, and they left it even before their arrest. The Minnesota Supreme Court, which overturned respondents' convictions, acknowledged that respondents could not be fairly characterized as Thompson's "guests." 569 N.W. 2d 169, 175–176 (1997). . . .

If respondents here had been visiting twenty homes, each for a minute or two, to drop off a bag of cocaine and were apprehended by a policeman wrongfully present in the nineteenth home; or if they had left the goods at a home where they were not staying and the police had seized the goods in their absence, we would have said that *Rakas* compels rejection of any privacy interest respondents might assert. So it does here, given that respondents have established no meaningful tie or connection to the owner, the owner's home, or the owner's expectation of privacy.

. . .

■ JUSTICE GINSBURG, with whom JUSTICE STEVENS and JUSTICE SOUTER join, dissenting.

The Court's decision undermines not only the security of short-term guests, but also the security of the home resident herself. In my view, when a homeowner or lessor personally invites a guest into her home to share in a common endeavor, whether it be for conversation, to engage in leisure activities, or for business purposes licit or illicit, that guest should share his host's shelter against unreasonable searches and seizures.

... I would here decide only the case of the homeowner who chooses to share the privacy of her home and her company with a guest, and would not reach classroom hypotheticals like the milkman or pizza deliverer.

My concern centers on an individual's choice to share her home and her associations there with persons she selects. Our decisions indicate that people have a reasonable expectation of privacy in their homes in part because they have the prerogative to exclude others.... The power to exclude implies the power to include.... Our Fourth Amendment decisions should reflect these complementary prerogatives.

A homedweller places her own privacy at risk, the Court's approach indicates, when she opens her home to others, uncertain whether the duration of their stay, their purpose, and their "acceptance into the household" will earn protection. Ante, at 90.... Human frailty suggests that today's decision will tempt police to pry into private dwellings without warrant, to find evidence incriminating guests who do not rest there through the night.... *Rakas* [v. Illinois, 439 U.S. 128 (1978)] tolerates that temptation with respect to automobile searches.... I see no impelling reason to extend this risk into the home.... As I see it, people are not genuinely "secure in their ... houses ... against unreasonable searches and seizures," U.S. Const., Amdt. 4, if their invitations to others increase the risk of unwarranted governmental peering and prying into their dwelling places.

Through the host's invitation, the guest gains a reasonable expectation of privacy in the home. Minnesota v. Olson, 495 U.S. 91 (1990), so held with respect to an overnight guest. The logic of that decision extends to shorter term guests as well.... Visiting the home of a friend, relative, or business associate, whatever the time of day, "serves functions recognized as valuable by society." *Olson*, 495 U.S., at 98. One need not remain overnight to anticipate privacy in another's home, "a place where [the guest] and his possessions will not be disturbed by anyone but his host and those his host allows inside." Id., at 99. In sum, when a homeowner chooses to share the privacy of her home and her company with a short-term guest, the twofold requirement "emerg[ing] from prior decisions" has been satisfied: Both host and guest "have exhibited an actual (subjective) expectation of privacy"; that "expectation [is] one [our] society is prepared to recognize as 'reasonable.' " Katz v. United States, 389 U.S. 347, 361 (1967) (Harlan, J., concurring).

As the Solicitor General acknowledged, the illegality of the host-guest conduct, the fact that they were partners in crime, would not alter the analysis. See Tr. of Oral Arg. 22–23.... Indeed, it must be this way. If the illegality of the activity made constitutional an otherwise unconstitutional search, such Fourth Amendment protection, reserved for the innocent only, would have little force in regulating police behavior toward either the innocent or the guilty.

Our leading decision in *Katz* is key to my view of this case. There, we ruled that the Government violated the petitioner's Fourth Amendment rights when it electronically recorded him transmitting wagering information while he was inside a public telephone booth. 389 U.S., at 353....

The Court's decision in this case veers sharply from the path marked in *Katz*. I do not agree that we have a more reasonable expectation of privacy when we place a business call to a person's home from a public telephone booth on the side of the street ... than when we actually enter that person's premises to engage in a common endeavor.

...[*]

Page 298

153. United States v. Husband, 312 F.3d 247 (7th Cir.2002) (intravenous administration of anesthetic that briefly rendered defendant unconscious, pursuant to warrant to search defendant's body, in order to remove drugs in plastic bags from his mouth upheld).

Page 303

158. United States v. McIver, 186 F.3d 1119 (9th Cir.1999) (tracking device placed on underside of car; *Knotts* followed).

Page 308

160. United States v. Long, 176 F.3d 1304 (10th Cir.1999) (defendant had no reasonable expectation of privacy in trash bags placed on top of a camper-trailer on his property near the property line, for pickup by trash collector).

[*] Justice Breyer wrote an opinion concurring in the judgment. He agreed with Justice Ginsburg, dissenting, that the defendants could claim the protection of the Fourth Amendment, but, on the basis of his own reading of the factual record, he concluded that the police officer's actions were not an unlawful search.

Page 325

United States v. Longoria, 177 F.3d 1179 (10th Cir.1999). The defendant conversed in Spanish with his codefendants while they were together talking with a government informant in the latter's shop. The informant secretly recorded the conversations, which were later introduced in evidence. The defendant believed that the informant did not understand Spanish. The defendant claimed that he had a "reasonable expectation of privacy" and, therefore, that the conversations were "oral communications" protected from disclosure under 18 U.S.C. §§ 2510(2), 2515. The court held that, despite his belief that the informant did not understand Spanish, his expectation of privacy was not one that the society is prepared to accept as reasonable.

Page 334

The Supreme Court of Vermont has held that a police officer's secret recording of a conversation he had with a person in the person's own home, without a judicially authorized warrant, violated the person's rights under the state constitution. State v. Geraw, 795 A.2d 1219 (2002). The court relied heavily on Justice Harlan's dissenting opinion in *White* and emphasized that the location of the recorded conversation may make a difference; the home, it said, is a place where the expectation of privacy is at its highest. The court observed further that the fact that the person spoke freely to the police officer does not indicate that he had no expectation of privacy so far as recording is concerned; otherwise the officer would not have recorded secretly.

Page 351

181. United States v. Mansoori, 304 F.3d 635 (7th Cir.2002) (basis for considering defendant's claim regarding minimization requirement not provided; claim not reached).

Page 354

187.

Kyllo v. United States

533 U.S. 27, 121 S.Ct. 2038, 150 L.Ed.2d 94 (2001).

■ JUSTICE SCALIA delivered the opinion of the Court.

This case presents the question whether the use of a thermal-imaging device aimed at a private home from a public street to detect relative amounts of heat within the home constitutes a "search" within the meaning of the Fourth Amendment.

I

In 1991 Agent William Elliott of the United States Department of the Interior came to suspect that marijuana was being grown in the home belonging to petitioner Danny Kyllo, part of a triplex on Rhododendron Drive in Florence, Oregon. Indoor marijuana growth typically requires high-intensity lamps. In order to determine whether an amount of heat was emanating from petitioner's home consistent with the use of such lamps, at 3:20 a.m. on January 16, 1992, Agent Elliott and Dan Haas used an Agema Thermovision 210 thermal imager to scan the triplex. Thermal imagers detect infrared radiation, which virtually all objects emit but which is not visible to the naked eye. The imager converts radiation into images based on relative warmth—black is cool, white is hot, shades of gray connote relative differences; in that respect, it operates somewhat like a video camera showing heat images. The scan of Kyllo's home took only a few minutes and was performed from the passenger seat of Agent Elliott's vehicle across the street from the front of the house and also from the street in back of the house. The scan showed that the roof over the garage and a side wall of petitioner's home were relatively hot compared to the rest of the home and substantially warmer than neighboring homes in the triplex. Agent Elliott concluded that petitioner was using halide lights to grow marijuana in his house, which indeed he was. Based on tips from informants, utility bills, and the thermal imaging, a Federal Magistrate Judge issued a warrant authorizing a search of petitioner's home, and the agents found an indoor growing operation involving more than 100 plants. Petitioner was indicted on one count of manufacturing marijuana, in violation of 21 U.S.C. § 841(a)(1). He unsuccessfully moved to suppress the evidence seized from his home and then entered a conditional guilty plea.

The Court of Appeals for the Ninth Circuit remanded the case for an evidentiary hearing regarding the intrusiveness of thermal imaging. On remand the District Court found that the Agema 210 "is a non-intrusive device which emits no rays or beams and shows a crude visual image of the heat being radiated from the outside of the house"; it "did not show any people or activity within the walls of the structure"; "[t]he device used cannot penetrate walls or windows to reveal conversations or human activities"; and "[n]o intimate details of the home were observed." Supp. App. to Pet. for Cert. 39–40. Based on these findings, the District Court upheld the validity of the warrant that relied in part upon the thermal imaging, and reaffirmed its denial of the motion to suppress. A divided Court of Appeals ... affirmed, 190 F.3d 1041 (1999), with Judge Noonan dissenting. The court held that petitioner had shown no subjective expectation of privacy because he had made no attempt to conceal the heat escaping from his home ... and even if he had, there was no objectively reasonable expectation of privacy because the imager "did not expose any intimate details of Kyllo's life," only "amorphous 'hot spots' on the roof and exterior wall," id., at 1047. We granted certiorari....

II

The Fourth Amendment provides that "[t]he right of the people to be secure in their persons, houses, papers, and effects, against unreasonable searches and seizures, shall not be violated." "At the very core" of the Fourth Amendment "stands the right of a man to retreat into his own home and there be free from unreasonable governmental intrusion." Silverman v. United States, 365 U.S. 505, 511 (1961). With few exceptions, the question whether a warrantless search of a home is reasonable and hence constitutional must be answered no. . . .

On the other hand, the antecedent question of whether or not a Fourth Amendment "search" has occurred is not so simple under our precedent. The permissibility of ordinary visual surveillance of a home used to be clear because, well into the 20th century, our Fourth Amendment jurisprudence was tied to common-law trespass. . . . We have since decoupled violation of a person's Fourth Amendment rights from trespassory violation of his property . . . but the lawfulness of warrantless visual surveillance of a home has still been preserved. . . .

One might think that the new validating rationale would be that examining the portion of a house that is in plain public view, while it is a "search" despite the absence of trespass, is not an "unreasonable" one under the Fourth Amendment. . . . But in fact we have held that visual observation is no "search" at all—perhaps in order to preserve somewhat more intact our doctrine that warrantless searches are presumptively unconstitutional. . . . In assessing when a search is not a search, we have applied somewhat in reverse the principle first enunciated in Katz v. United States, 389 U.S. 347 (1967). *Katz* involved eavesdropping by means of an electronic listening device placed on the outside of a telephone booth—a location not within the catalog ("persons, houses, papers, and effects") that the Fourth Amendment protects against unreasonable searches. We held that the Fourth Amendment nonetheless protected Katz from the warrantless eavesdropping because he "justifiably relied" upon the privacy of the telephone booth. Id., at 353. As Justice Harlan's oft-quoted concurrence described it, a Fourth Amendment search occurs when the government violates a subjective expectation of privacy that society recognizes as reasonable. See id., at 361. We have subsequently applied this principle to hold that a Fourth Amendment search does *not* occur—even when the explicitly protected location of a *house* is concerned—unless "the individual manifested a subjective expectation of privacy in the object of the challenged search," and "society [is] willing to recognize that expectation as reasonable." [California v.] *Ciraolo*, [476 U.S. 207 (1986)], at 211. . . .

The present case involves officers on a public street engaged in more than naked-eye surveillance of a home. We have previously reserved judgment as to how much technological enhancement of ordinary perception from such a vantage point, if any, is too much. . . .

III

It would be foolish to contend that the degree of privacy secured to citizens by the Fourth Amendment has been entirely unaffected by the advance of technology. For example, as the cases discussed above make clear, the technology enabling human flight has exposed to public view (and hence, we have said, to official observation) uncovered portions of the house and its curtilage that once were private.... The question we confront today is what limits there are upon this power of technology to shrink the realm of guaranteed privacy.

The *Katz* test—whether the individual has an expectation of privacy that society is prepared to recognize as reasonable—has often been criticized as circular, and hence subjective and unpredictable.... While it may be difficult to refine *Katz* when the search of areas such as telephone booths, automobiles, or even the curtilage and uncovered portions of residences are at issue, in the case of the search of the interior of homes—the prototypical and hence most commonly litigated area of protected privacy—there is a ready criterion, with roots deep in the common law, of the minimal expectation of privacy that *exists*, and that is acknowledged to be *reasonable*. To withdraw protection of this minimum expectation would be to permit police technology to erode the privacy guaranteed by the Fourth Amendment. We think that obtaining by sense-enhancing technology any information regarding the interior of the home that could not otherwise have been obtained without physical "intrusion into a constitutionally protected area," *Silverman* [v. United States], 365 U.S. [505 (1961)], at 512, constitutes a search—at least where (as here) the technology in question is not in general public use. This assures preservation of that degree of privacy against government that existed when the Fourth Amendment was adopted. On the basis of this criterion, the information obtained by the thermal imager in this case was the product of a search.

The Government maintains, however, that the thermal imaging must be upheld because it detected "only heat radiating from the external surface of the house," Brief for United States 26. The dissent makes this its leading point ... contending that there is a fundamental difference between what it calls "off-the-wall" observations and "through-the-wall surveillance." But just as a thermal imager captures only heat emanating from a house, so also a powerful directional microphone picks up only sound emanating from a house—and a satellite capable of scanning from many miles away would pick up only visible light emanating from a house. We rejected such a mechanical interpretation of the Fourth Amendment in *Katz*, where the eavesdropping device picked up only sound waves that reached the exterior of the phone booth. Reversing that approach would leave the homeowner at the mercy of advancing technology—including imaging technology that could discern all human activity in the home. While the technology used in the present case was relatively crude, the rule we adopt must take account of more sophisticated systems that are already in use or in development. The dissent's reliance on the distinction between "off-the-wall" and "through-the-wall" observation is entirely incompatible with the dissent's belief, which we discuss below, that thermal-imaging observations of the intimate details of a home are impermissible. The most sophisticated thermal imaging devices continue to measure heat "off-the-wall" rather than "through-the-wall"; the dissent's disapproval of those more sophisticated thermal-imaging devices ... is an acknowledgement that there is no substance to this distinction. As for the dissent's extraordinary assertion that anything learned through "an inference" cannot be a search ... that would validate even the "through-the-wall" technologies that the dissent purports to disapprove. Surely the dissent does not believe that the through-the-wall radar or ultrasound technology produces an 8–by–10 Kodak glossy that needs no analysis (i.e., the making of inferences)....

The Government also contends that the thermal imaging was constitutional because it did not "detect private activities occurring in private areas," Brief for United States 22. It points out that in *Dow Chemical* we observed that the enhanced aerial photography did not reveal any "intimate details." [Dow Chemical Co. v. United States,] 476 U.S. [227 (1986)], at 238. *Dow Chemical*, however, involved enhanced aerial photography of an industrial complex, which does not share the Fourth Amendment sanctity of the home.... In the home, our cases show, *all* details are intimate details, because the entire area is held safe from prying government eyes....

Limiting the prohibition of thermal imaging to "intimate details" would not only be wrong in principle; it would be impractical in application, failing to provide "a workable accommodation between the needs of law enforcement and the interests protected by the Fourth Amendment," Oliver v. United States, 466 U.S. 170, 181 (1984). To begin with, there is no necessary connection between the sophistication of the surveillance equipment and the "intimacy" of the details that it observes—which means that one cannot say (and the police cannot be assured) that use of the relatively crude equipment at issue here will always be lawful. The Agema Thermovision 210 might disclose, for example, at what hour each night the lady of the house takes her daily sauna and bath—a detail that many would consider "intimate"; and a much more sophisticated system might detect nothing more intimate than the fact that someone left a closet light on. We could not, in other words, develop a rule approving only that through-the-wall surveillance which identifies objects no smaller than 36 by 36 inches, but would have to develop a jurisprudence specifying which home activities are "intimate" and which are not. And even when (if ever) that jurisprudence were fully developed, no police officer would be able to know *in advance* whether his through-the-wall surveillance picks up "intimate" details—and thus would be unable to know in advance whether it is constitutional.

The dissent's proposed standard—whether the technology offers the "functional equivalent of actual presence in the area being searched," post, at 47—would seem quite similar to our own at first blush. The dissent concludes that *Katz* was such a case, but then inexplicably asserts that if the same listening device only revealed the volume of the conversation, the surveillance would be permissible. . . . Yet if, without technology, the police could not discern volume without being actually present in the phone booth, Justice Stevens should conclude a search has occurred. . . . The same should hold for the interior heat of the home if only a person present in the home could discern the heat. Thus the driving force of the dissent, despite its recitation of the above standard, appears to be a distinction among different types of information—whether the "homeowner would even care if anybody noticed," post, at 49. The dissent offers no practical guidance for the application of this standard, and for reasons already discussed, we believe there can be none. The people in their houses, as well as the police, deserve more precision.

We have said that the Fourth Amendment draws "a firm line at the entrance to the house," *Payton* [v. New York], 445 U.S. [573 (1980)], at 590. That line, we think, must be not only firm but also bright—which requires clear specification of those methods of surveillance that require a warrant. While it is certainly possible to conclude from the videotape of the thermal imaging that occurred in this case that no "significant" compromise of the homeowner's privacy has occurred, we must take the long view, from the original meaning of the Fourth Amendment forward. . . . Where, as here, the Government uses a device that is not in general public use, to explore details of the home that would previously have been unknowable without physical intrusion, the surveillance is a "search" and is presumptively unreasonable without a warrant.

Since we hold the Thermovision imaging to have been an unlawful search, it will remain for the District Court to determine whether, without the evidence it provided, the search warrant issued in this case was supported by probable cause—and if not, whether there is any other basis for supporting admission of the evidence that the search pursuant to the warrant produced.

. . .

■ JUSTICE STEVENS, with whom THE CHIEF JUSTICE, JUSTICE O'CONNOR, and JUSTICE KENNEDY join, dissenting.

There is, in my judgment, a distinction of constitutional magnitude between "through-the-wall surveillance" that gives the observer or listener direct access to information in a private area, on the one hand, and the thought processes used to draw inferences from information in the public domain, on the other hand. The Court has crafted a rule that purports to deal with direct observations of the inside of the home, but the case before us merely involves indirect deductions from "off-the-wall" surveillance, that is, observations of the exterior of the home. Those observations were made with a fairly primitive thermal imager that gathered data exposed on the outside of petitioner's home but did not invade any constitutionally protected interest in privacy. Moreover, I believe that the supposedly "bright-line" rule the Court has created in response to its concerns about future technological developments is unnecessary, unwise, and inconsistent with the Fourth Amendment.

I

There is no need for the Court to craft a new rule to decide this case, as it is controlled by established principles from our Fourth Amendment jurisprudence. One of those core principles, of course, is that "searches and seizures *inside a home* without a warrant are presumptively unreasonable." Payton v. New York, 445 U.S. 573, 586 (1980) (emphasis added). But it is equally well settled that searches and seizures of property in plain view are presumptively reasonable.... Whether that property is residential or commercial, the basic principle is the same: " 'What a person knowingly exposes to the public, even in his own home or office, is not a subject of Fourth Amendment protection.' " California v. Ciraolo, 476 U.S. 207, 213 (1986) (quoting Katz v. United States, 389 U.S. 347, 351 (1967)).... That is the principle implicated here.

While the Court "take[s] the long view" and decides this case based largely on the potential of yet-to-be-developed technology that might allow "through-the-wall surveillance," ante, at 38–40, ... this case involves nothing more than off-the-wall surveillance by law enforcement officers to gather information exposed to the general public from the outside of petitioner's home. All that the infrared camera did in this case was passively measure heat emitted from the exterior surfaces of petitioner's home; all that those measurements showed were relative differences in emission levels, vaguely indicating that some areas of the roof and outside walls were warmer than others. As still images from the infrared scans show ... no details regarding the interior of petitioner's home were revealed. Unlike an x-ray scan, or other possible "through-the-wall" techniques, the detection of infrared radiation emanating from the home did not accomplish "an unauthorized physical penetration into the premises," Silverman v. United States, 365 U.S. 505, 509 (1961), nor did it "obtain information that it could not have obtained by observation from outside the curtilage of the house," United States v. Karo, 468 U.S. 705, 715 (1984).

Indeed, the ordinary use of the senses might enable a neighbor or passerby to notice the heat emanating from a building, particularly if it is vented, as was the case here. Additionally, any member of the public might notice that one part of a house is warmer than another part or a nearby building if, for example, rainwater evaporates or snow melts at different rates across its surfaces. Such use of the senses would not convert into an unreasonable search if, instead, an adjoining neighbor allowed an officer onto her property to verify her perceptions with a sensitive thermometer. Nor, in my view, does such observation become an unreasonable search if made from a distance with the aid of a device that merely discloses that the exterior of one house, or one area of the house, is much warmer than another. Nothing more occurred in this case.

Thus, the notion that heat emissions from the outside of a dwelling is a private matter implicating the protections of the Fourth Amendment (the text of which guarantees the right of people "to be secure *in* their . . . houses" against unreasonable searches and seizures (emphasis added)) is not only unprecedented but also quite difficult to take seriously. Heat waves, like aromas that are generated in a kitchen, or in a laboratory or opium den, enter the public domain if and when they leave a building. A subjective expectation that they would remain private is not only implausible but also surely not "one that society is prepared to recognize as 'reasonable.' " *Katz*, 389 U.S., at 361 (Harlan, J., concurring).

To be sure, the homeowner has a reasonable expectation of privacy concerning what takes place within the home, and the Fourth Amendment's protection against physical invasions of the home should apply to their functional equivalent. But the equipment in this case did not penetrate the walls of petitioner's home, and while it did pick up "details of the home" that were exposed to the public, ante, at 38, it did not obtain "any information regarding the *interior* of the home," ante, at 40 (emphasis added). In the Court's own words, based on what the thermal imager "showed" regarding the outside of petitioner's home, the officers "concluded" that petitioner was engaging in illegal activity inside the home. Ante, at 30. It would be quite absurd to characterize their thought processes as "searches," regardless of whether they inferred (rightly) that petitioner was growing marijuana in his house, or (wrongly) that "the lady of the house [was taking] her daily sauna and bath." Ante, at 38. . . . For the first time in its history, the Court assumes that an inference can amount to a Fourth Amendment violation. See ante, at 36–37.

Notwithstanding the implications of today's decision, there is a strong public interest in avoiding constitutional litigation over the monitoring of emissions from homes, and over the inferences drawn from such monitoring. Just as "the police cannot reasonably be expected to avert their eyes from evidence of criminal activity that could have been observed by any member of the public," [California v.] *Greenwood*, 486 U.S. [35 (1988)], at 41, so too public officials should not have to avert their senses or their equipment from detecting emissions in the public domain such as excessive heat, traces of smoke, suspicious odors, odorless gases, airborne particulates, or radioactive emissions, any of which could identify hazards to the community. In my judgment, monitoring such emissions with "sense-enhancing technology," ante, at 34, and drawing useful conclusions from such monitoring, is an entirely reasonable public service.

On the other hand, the countervailing privacy interest is at best trivial. After all, homes generally are insulated to keep heat in, rather than to prevent the detection of heat going out, and it does not seem to me that society will suffer from a rule requiring the rare homeowner who both intends to engage in uncommon activities that produce extraordinary amounts of heat, and wishes to conceal that production from outsiders, to make sure that the surrounding area is well insulated.... The interest in concealing the heat escaping from one's house pales in significance to the "the chief evil against which the wording of the Fourth Amendment is directed," the "physical entry of the home," United States v. United States Dist. Court for Eastern Dist. of Mich., 407 U.S. 297, 313 (1972), and it is hard to believe that it is an interest the Framers sought to protect in our Constitution.

Since what was involved in this case was nothing more than drawing inferences from off-the-wall surveillance, rather than any "through-the-wall" surveillance, the officers' conduct did not amount to a search and was perfectly reasonable.

II

Instead of trying to answer the question whether the use of the thermal imager in this case was even arguably unreasonable, the Court has fashioned a rule that is intended to provide essential guidance for the day when "more sophisticated systems" gain the "ability to 'see' through walls and other opaque barriers." Ante, at 36, and n. 3. The newly minted rule encompasses "obtaining [1] by sense-enhancing technology [2] any information regarding the interior of the home [3] that could not otherwise have been obtained without physical intrusion into a constitutionally protected area ... [4] at least where (as here) the technology in question is not in general public use." Ante, at 34 (internal quotation marks omitted). In my judgment, the Court's new rule is at once too broad and too narrow, and is not justified by the Court's explanation for its adoption. As I have suggested, I would not erect a constitutional impediment to the use of sense-enhancing technology unless it provides its user with the functional equivalent of actual presence in the area being searched.

Despite the Court's attempt to draw a line that is "not only firm but also bright," ante, at 40, the contours of its new rule are uncertain because its protection apparently dissipates as soon as the relevant technology is "in general public use," ante, at 34. Yet how much use is general public use is not even hinted at by the Court's opinion, which makes the somewhat doubtful assumption that the thermal imager used in this case does not satisfy that criterion. In any event, putting aside its lack of clarity, this criterion is somewhat perverse because it seems likely that the threat to privacy will grow, rather than recede, as the use of intrusive equipment becomes more readily available.

It is clear, however, that the category of "sense-enhancing technology" covered by the new rule, ibid. is far too broad. It would, for example, embrace potential mechanical substitutes for dogs trained to react when they sniff narcotics. But in United States v. Place, 462 U.S. 696, 707 (1983), we held that a dog sniff that "discloses only the presence or absence of narcotics" does "not constitute a 'search' within the meaning of the Fourth Amendment," and it must follow that sense-enhancing equipment that identifies nothing but illegal activity is not a search either. Nevertheless, the use of such a device would be unconstitutional under the Court's rule, as would the use of other new devices that might detect the odor of deadly bacteria or chemicals for making a new type of high explosive, even if the devices (like the dog sniffs) are "so limited in both the manner in which" they obtain information and "in the content of the information" they reveal. Ibid. If nothing more than that sort of information could be obtained by using the devices in a public place to monitor emissions from a house, then their use would be no more objectionable than the use of the thermal imager in this case.

The application of the Court's new rule to "any information regarding the interior of the home," ante, at 34, is also unnecessarily broad. If it takes sensitive equipment to detect an odor that identifies criminal conduct and nothing else, the fact that the odor emanates from the interior of a home should not provide it with constitutional protection. See supra, at 47. The criterion, moreover, is too sweeping in that information "regarding" the interior of a home apparently is not just information obtained through its walls, but also information concerning the outside of the building that could lead to (however many) inferences "regarding" what might be inside. Under that expansive view, I suppose, an officer using an infrared camera to observe a man silently entering the side door of a house at night carrying a pizza might conclude that its interior is now occupied by someone who likes pizza, and by doing so the officer would be guilty of conducting an unconstitutional "search" of the home.

Because the new rule applies to information regarding the "interior" of the home, it is too narrow as well as too broad. Clearly, a rule that is designed to protect individuals from the overly intrusive use of sense-enhancing equipment should not be limited to a home. If such equipment did provide its user with the functional equivalent of access to a private place—such as, for example, the telephone booth involved in *Katz*, or an office building—then the rule should apply to such an area as well as to a home. See *Katz*, 389 U.S., at 351. . . .

The final requirement of the Court's new rule, that the information "could not otherwise have been obtained without physical intrusion into a constitutionally protected area," ante, at 34 (internal quotation marks omitted), also extends too far as the Court applies it. As noted, the Court effectively treats the mental process of analyzing data obtained from external sources as the equivalent of a physical intrusion into the home. . . . As I have explained, however, the process of drawing inferences from data in the public domain should not be characterized as a search.

The two reasons advanced by the Court as justifications for the adoption of its new rule are both unpersuasive. First, the Court suggests that its rule is compelled by our holding in *Katz*, because in that case, as in this, the surveillance consisted of nothing more than the monitoring of waves emanating from a private area into the public domain. . . . Yet there are critical differences between the cases. In *Katz*, the electronic listening device attached to the outside of the phone booth allowed the officers to pick up the content of the conversation inside the booth, making them the functional equivalent of intruders because they gathered information that was otherwise available only to someone inside the private area; it would be as if, in this case, the thermal imager presented a view of the heat-generating activity inside petitioner's home. By contrast, the thermal imager here disclosed only the relative amounts of heat radiating from the house; it would be as if, in *Katz*, the listening device disclosed only the relative volume of sound leaving the booth, which presumably was discernible in the public domain. Surely, there is a significant difference between the general and well-settled expectation that strangers will not have direct access to the contents of private communications, on the one hand, and the rather theoretical expectation that an occasional homeowner would even care if anybody noticed the relative amounts of heat emanating from the walls of his house, on the other. It is pure hyperbole for the Court to suggest that refusing to extend the holding of *Katz* to this case would leave the homeowner at the mercy of "technology that could discern all human activity in the home." Ante, at 35–36.

Second, the Court argues that the permissibility of "through-the-wall surveillance" cannot depend on a distinction between observing "intimate details" such as "the lady of the house [taking] her daily sauna and bath," and noticing only "the nonintimate rug on the vestibule floor" or "objects no smaller than 36 by 36 inches." Ante, at 37, 38–39. This entire argument assumes, of course, that the thermal imager in this case could or did perform "through-the-wall surveillance" that could identify any detail "that would previously have been unknowable without physical intrusion." Ante, at 39–40. In fact, the device could not . . . and did not . . . enable its user to identify either the lady of the house, the rug on the vestibule floor, or anything else inside the house, whether smaller or larger than 36 by 36 inches. Indeed, the vague thermal images of petitioner's home . . . were submitted by him to the District Court as part of an expert report raising the question whether the device could even take "accurate, consistent infrared images" of the *outside* of his house. Defendant's Exhibit 107, p. 4. But even if the device could reliably show extraordinary differences in the amounts of heat leaving his home, drawing the inference that there was something suspicious occurring inside the residence—a conclusion that officers far less gifted than Sherlock Holmes would readily draw—does not qualify as "through-the-wall surveillance," much less a Fourth Amendment violation.

III

Although the Court is properly and commendably concerned about the threats to privacy that may flow from advances in the technology available to the law enforcement profession, it has unfortunately failed to heed the tried and true counsel of judicial restraint. Instead of concentrating on the rather mundane issue that is actually presented by the case before it, the Court has endeavored to craft an all-encompassing rule for the future. It would be far wiser to give legislators an unimpeded opportunity to grapple with these emerging issues rather than to shackle them with prematurely devised constitutional constraints.

. . .

CHAPTER 5

Examination and Identification

Page 368

193. State v. Ravotto, 777 A.2d 301 (N.J.2001) (unreasonable force used to obtain blood sample from person arrested for drunk driving; evidence suppressed).

See supplement to page 298 note 153, above.

194. Relying on Schmerber v. California (Casebook, p. 361), the Supreme Court of South Dakota held that the taking of a urine sample of an arrested person without her consent did not violate the defendant's rights under the Fourth Amendment. State v. Hanson, 588 N.W.2d 885 (S.D.1999).

Page 373

202. See Penry v. Johnson, 532 U.S. 782 (2001).

Page 401

United States v. Guevara-Martinez, 262 F.3d 751 (8th Cir.2001) (*Davis* and *Hayes* applied).

CHAPTER 6

QUESTIONING

Page 417

228. United States v. Hayes, 231 F.3d 663 (9th Cir.2000) (en banc). During an investigation of a scheme to sell college grades to foreign students, the government took material witness depositions of some students so that they could go home. The defendant, who was a suspect in the investigation, was notified that the depositions would be taken and obtained counsel. Thereafter, but before he was indicted, the government secretly taped a conversation of the defendant with a co-conspirator, with the latter's cooperation. Adhering to the rule that the right to counsel attaches after the formal initiation of criminal proceedings, the majority held that the taped conversation was admissible. Dissenting judges argued that the taking of the depositions for use at trial brought the right to counsel into play. (They noted that it was questionable whether it was proper under Rule 15, Fed. R. Crim. P., to authorize the taking of material witness depositions before indictment. The government in the end did not use the depositions at the trial.)

Page 418

Texas v. Cobb

532 U.S. 162, 121 S.Ct. 1335, 149 L.Ed.2d 321 (2001).

■ CHIEF JUSTICE REHNQUIST delivered the opinion of the Court.

The Texas Court of Criminal Appeals held that a criminal defendant's Sixth Amendment right to counsel attaches not only to the offense with which he is charged, but to other offenses "closely related factually" to the charged offense. We hold that our decision in McNeil v. Wisconsin, 501 U.S. 171 (1991), meant what it said, and that the Sixth Amendment right is "offense specific."

In December 1993, Lindsey Owings reported to the Walker County, Texas, Sheriff's Office that the home he shared with his wife, Margaret, and their 16-month-old daughter, Kori Rae, had been burglarized. He also informed police that his wife and daughter were missing. Respondent Raymond Levi Cobb lived across the street from the Owings. Acting on an anonymous tip that respondent was involved in the burglary, Walker

County investigators questioned him about the events. He denied involvement. In July 1994, while under arrest for an unrelated offense, respondent was again questioned about the incident. Respondent then gave a written statement confessing to the burglary, but he denied knowledge relating to the disappearances. Respondent was subsequently indicted for the burglary, and Hal Ridley was appointed in August 1994 to represent respondent on that charge.

Shortly after Ridley's appointment, investigators asked and received his permission to question respondent about the disappearances. Respondent continued to deny involvement. Investigators repeated this process in September 1995, again with Ridley's permission and again with the same result.

In November 1995, respondent, free on bond in the burglary case, was living with his father in Odessa, Texas. At that time, respondent's father contacted the Walker County Sheriff's Office to report that respondent had confessed to him that he killed Margaret Owings in the course of the burglary. Walker County investigators directed respondent's father to the Odessa police station, where he gave a statement. Odessa police then faxed the statement to Walker County, where investigators secured a warrant for respondent's arrest and faxed it back to Odessa. Shortly thereafter, Odessa police took respondent into custody and administered warnings pursuant to Miranda v. Arizona, 384 U.S. 436 (1966). Respondent waived these rights.

After a short time, respondent confessed to murdering both Margaret and Kori Rae. Respondent explained that when Margaret confronted him as he was attempting to remove the Owings' stereo, he stabbed her in the stomach with a knife he was carrying. Respondent told police that he dragged her body to a wooded area a few hundred yards from the house. Respondent then stated:

> "I went back to her house and I saw the baby laying on its bed. I took the baby out there and it was sleeping the whole time. I laid the baby down on the ground four or five feet away from its mother. I went back to my house and got a flat edge shovel. That's all I could find. Then I went back over to where they were and I started digging a hole between them. After I got the hole dug, the baby was awake. It started going toward its mom and it fell in the hole. I put the lady in the hole and I covered them up. I remember stabbing a different knife I had in the ground where they were. I was crying right then." App. to Pet. for Cert. A–9 to A–10.

Respondent later led police to the location where he had buried the victims' bodies.

Respondent was convicted of capital murder for murdering more than one person in the course of a single criminal transaction.... He was sentenced to death. On appeal to the Court of Criminal Appeals of Texas, respondent argued, *inter alia*, that his confession should have been suppressed because it was obtained in violation of his Sixth Amendment right to counsel. Relying on Michigan v. Jackson, 475 U.S. 625 (1986), respondent contended that his right to counsel had attached when Ridley was appointed in the burglary case and that Odessa police were therefore required to secure Ridley's permission before proceeding with the interrogation.

The Court of Criminal Appeals reversed respondent's conviction by a divided vote and remanded for a new trial. The court held that "once the right to counsel attaches to the offense charged, it also attaches to any other offense that is very closely related factually to the offense charged." 2000 WL 275641, *3 (2000) (citations omitted). Finding the capital murder charge to be "factually interwoven with the burglary," the court concluded that respondent's Sixth Amendment right to counsel had attached on the capital murder charge even though respondent had not yet been charged with that offense. Id., at *4. The court further found that respondent had asserted that right by accepting Ridley's appointment in the burglary case.... Accordingly, it deemed the confession inadmissible and found that its introduction had not been harmless error.... Three justices dissented, finding Michigan v. Jackson to be distinguishable and concluding that respondent had made a valid unilateral waiver of his right to counsel before confessing....

The State sought review in this Court, and we granted certiorari to consider ... whether the Sixth Amendment right to counsel extends to crimes that are "factually related" to those that have actually been charged....

The Sixth Amendment provides that "[i]n all criminal prosecutions, the accused shall enjoy the right ... to have the Assistance of Counsel for his defence." In McNeil v. Wisconsin, 501 U.S. 171 (1991), we explained when this right arises ... [W]e held that a defendant's statements regarding offenses for which he had not been charged were admissible notwithstanding the attachment of his Sixth Amendment right to counsel on other charged offenses....

Some state courts and Federal Courts of Appeals, however, have read into *McNeil's* offense-specific definition an exception for crimes that are "factually related" to a charged offense.... We decline to do so.

. . .

Respondent predicts that the offense-specific rule will prove "disastrous" to suspects' constitutional rights and will "permit law enforcement officers almost complete and total license to conduct unwanted and uncounseled interrogations." Brief for Respondent 8–9. Besides offering no evidence that such a parade of horribles has occurred in those jurisdictions that have not enlarged upon *McNeil*, he fails to appreciate the significance of two critical considerations. First, there can be no doubt that a suspect must be apprised of his rights against compulsory self-incrimination and to consult with an attorney before authorities may conduct custodial interrogation.... In the present case, police scrupulously followed *Miranda*'s dictates when questioning respondent.[2] Second, it is critical to recognize that the Constitution does not negate society's interest in the ability of police to talk to witnesses and suspects, even those who have been charged with other offenses....

Although it is clear that the Sixth Amendment right to counsel attaches only to charged offenses, we have recognized in other contexts that the definition of an "offense" is not necessarily limited to the four corners of a charging instrument. In Blockburger v. United States, 284 U.S. 299 (1932), we explained that "where the same act or transaction constitutes a violation of two distinct statutory provisions, the test to be applied to determine whether there are two offenses or only one, is whether each provision requires proof of a fact which the other does not." Id., at 304. We have since applied the *Blockburger* test to delineate the scope of the Fifth Amendment's Double Jeopardy Clause, which prevents multiple or successive prosecutions for the "same offence." See, *e.g.*, Brown v. Ohio, 432 U.S. 161, 164–166 (1977). We see no constitutional difference between the meaning of the term "offense" in the contexts of double jeopardy and of the right to counsel. Accordingly, we hold that when the Sixth Amendment right to counsel attaches, it does encompass offenses that, even if not formally charged, would be considered the same offense under the *Blockburger* test.

While simultaneously conceding that its own test "lacks the precision for which police officers may hope," post, at 186, the dissent suggests that adopting *Blockburger*'s definition of "offense" will prove difficult to administer. But it is the dissent's vague iterations of the " 'closely related to' " or

2. Curiously, while predicting disastrous consequences for the core values underlying the Sixth Amendment ... the dissenters give short shrift to the Fifth Amendment's role ... in protecting a defendant's right to consult with counsel before talking to police. Even though the Sixth Amendment right to counsel has not attached to uncharged offenses, defendants retain the ability under *Miranda* to refuse any police questioning, and, indeed, charged defendants presumably have met with counsel and have had the opportunity to discuss whether it is advisable to invoke those Fifth Amendment rights. Thus, in all but the rarest of cases, the Court's decision today will have no impact whatsoever upon a defendant's ability to protect his Sixth Amendment right.

It is also worth noting that, contrary to the dissent's suggestion ... there is no "background principle" of our Sixth Amendment jurisprudence establishing that there may be no contact between a defendant and police without counsel present. The dissent would expand the Sixth Amendment right to the assistance of counsel in a criminal prosecution into a rule which " 'exists to prevent lawyers from taking advantage of uncounseled laypersons and to preserve the integrity of the lawyer-client relationship.' " Post, at 181 (quoting ABA Ann. Model Rule of Professional Conduct 4.2 (4th ed.1999)). Every profession is competent to define the standards of conduct for its members, but such standards are obviously not controlling in interpretation of constitutional provisions. The Sixth Amendment right to counsel is personal to the defendant and specific to the offense.

" 'inextricably intertwined with' " test, post, at 186, that would defy simple application. The dissent seems to presuppose that officers will possess complete knowledge of the circumstances surrounding an incident, such that the officers will be able to tailor their investigation to avoid addressing factually related offenses. Such an assumption, however, ignores the reality that police often are not yet aware of the exact sequence and scope of events they are investigating—indeed, that is why police must investigate in the first place. Deterred by the possibility of violating the Sixth Amendment, police likely would refrain from questioning certain defendants altogether.

It remains only to apply these principles to the facts at hand. At the time he confessed to Odessa police, respondent had been indicted for burglary of the Owings residence, but he had not been charged in the murders of Margaret and Kori Rae. As defined by Texas law, burglary and capital murder are not the same offense under *Blockburger*. ... Accordingly, the Sixth Amendment right to counsel did not bar police from interrogating respondent regarding the murders, and respondent's confession was therefore admissible.

. . .

■ JUSTICE BREYER, with whom JUSTICE STEVENS, JUSTICE SOUTER, and JUSTICE GINSBURG join, dissenting.

This case focuses upon the meaning of a single word, "offense," when it arises in the context of the Sixth Amendment. Several basic background principles define that context.

First, the Sixth Amendment right to counsel plays a central role in ensuring the fairness of criminal proceedings in our system of justice....

Second, the right attaches when adversary proceedings, triggered by the government's formal accusation of a crime, begin....

Third, once this right attaches, law enforcement officials are required, in most circumstances, to deal with the defendant through counsel rather than directly, even if the defendant has waived his Fifth Amendment rights....

Fourth, the particular aspect of the right here at issue—the rule that the police ordinarily must communicate with the defendant through counsel—has important limits. In particular, recognizing the need for law enforcement officials to investigate "new or additional crimes" not the subject of current proceedings, Maine v. Moulton, [474 U.S. 159 (1985)] at 179, this Court has made clear that the right to counsel does not attach to any and every crime that an accused may commit or have committed.... The right "cannot be invoked once for all future prosecutions," and it does not forbid "interrogation unrelated to the charge." [McNeil v. Wisconsin, 501 U.S. 171 (1991)], at 175, 178. In a word, as this Court previously noted, the right is "offense specific." Id., at 175.

This case focuses upon the last-mentioned principle, in particular upon the meaning of the words "offense specific." ... This case requires us to determine whether an "offense"—for Sixth Amendment purposes—includes factually related aspects of a single course of conduct other than those few acts that make up the essential elements of the crime charged.

We should answer this question in light of the Sixth Amendment's basic objectives as set forth in this Court's case law. At the very least, we should answer it in a way that does not undermine those objectives. But the Court today decides that "offense" means the crime set forth within "the four corners of a charging instrument," along with other crimes that "would be considered the same offense" under the test established by Blockburger v. United States, 284 U.S. 299 (1932). Ante, at 173. In my view, this unnecessarily technical definition undermines Sixth Amendment protections while doing nothing to further effective law enforcement.

For one thing, the majority's rule, while leaving the Fifth Amendment's protections in place, threatens to diminish severely the additional protection that, under this Court's rulings, the Sixth Amendment provides when it grants the right to counsel to defendants who have been charged with a crime and insists that law enforcement officers thereafter communicate with them through that counsel. ...

. . .

... [T]he Sixth Amendment right at issue is independent of the Fifth Amendment's protections; and the importance of this Sixth Amendment right has been repeatedly recognized in our cases. ...

. . .

... [C]riminal codes are lengthy and highly detailed, often proliferating "overlapping and related statutory offenses" to the point where prosecutors can easily "spin out a startlingly numerous series of offenses from a single ... criminal transaction." Ashe v. Swenson, 397 U.S. 436, 445, n.10 (1970). Thus, an armed robber who reaches across a store counter, grabs the cashier, and demands "your money or your life," may through that single instance of conduct have committed several "offenses," in the majority's sense of the term, including armed robbery, assault, battery, trespass, use of a firearm to commit a felony, and perhaps possession of a firearm by a felon, as well. A person who is using and selling drugs on a single occasion might be guilty of possessing various drugs, conspiring to sell drugs, being under the influence of illegal drugs, possessing drug paraphernalia, possessing a gun in relation to the drug sale, and, depending upon circumstances, violating various gun laws as well. A protester blocking an entrance to a federal building might also be trespassing, failing to disperse, unlawfully assembling, and obstructing Government administration all at one and the same time.

The majority's rule permits law enforcement officials to question those charged with a crime without first approaching counsel, through the simple device of asking questions about any other related crime not actually charged in the indictment. Thus, the police could ask the individual charged with robbery about, say, the assault of the cashier not yet charged, or about any other uncharged offense (unless under *Blockburger*'s definition it counts as the "same crime"), all *without notifying counsel.* Indeed, the majority's rule would permit law enforcement officials to question anyone charged with any crime in any one of the examples just given about his or her conduct on the single relevant occasion without notifying counsel unless the prosecutor has charged every possible crime arising out of that same brief course of conduct. What Sixth Amendment sense—what common sense—does such a rule make? What is left of the "communicate through counsel" rule? The majority's approach is inconsistent with any common understanding of the scope of counsel's representation. It will undermine the lawyer's role as " 'medium' " between the defendant and the government. Maine v. Moulton, supra, at 176. And it will, on a random basis, remove a significant portion of the protection that this Court has found inherent in the Sixth Amendment.

. . .

At the same time, the majority's rule threatens the legal clarity necessary for effective law enforcement. That is because the majority, aware that the word "offense" ought to encompass something beyond "the four corners of the charging instrument," imports into Sixth Amendment law the definition of "offense" set forth in Blockburger v. United States, 284 U.S. 299 (1932), a case interpreting the Double Jeopardy Clause of the Fifth Amendment, which Clause uses the word "offence" but otherwise has no relevance here. Whatever Fifth Amendment virtues *Blockburger* may have, to import it into this Sixth Amendment context will work havoc.

In theory, the test says that two offenses are the "same offense" unless each requires proof of a fact that the other does not. See ante, at 173 (majority opinion). That means that most of the different crimes mentioned above are not the "same offense." Under many States' laws, for example, the statute defining assault and the statute defining robbery each requires proof of a fact that the other does not.... Hence the extension of the definition of "offense" that is accomplished by the use of the *Blockburger* test does nothing to address the substantial concerns about the circumvention of the Sixth Amendment right that are raised by the majority's rule.

But, more to the point, the simple-sounding *Blockburger* test has proved extraordinarily difficult to administer in practice. ...

There is, of course, an alternative. We can, and should, define "offense" in terms of the conduct that constitutes the crime that the offender committed on a particular occasion, including criminal acts that are "closely related to" or "inextricably intertwined with" the particular crime set forth in the charging instrument. This alternative is not perfect. The language used lacks the precision for which police officers may hope; and it requires lower courts to specify its meaning further as they apply it in individual cases. Yet virtually every lower court in the United States to consider the issue has defined "offense" in the Sixth Amendment context to encompass such closely related acts....

One cannot say in favor of this commonly followed approach that it is perfectly clear—only that, because it comports with common sense, it is far easier to apply than that of the majority. One might add that, unlike the majority's test, it is consistent with this Court's assumptions in previous cases.... And, most importantly, the "closely related" test furthers, rather than undermines, the Sixth Amendment's "right to counsel," a right so necessary to the realization in practice of that most "noble ideal," a fair trial. Gideon v. Wainwright, 372 U.S. [335 (1963)], at 344.

The Texas Court of Criminal Appeals, following this commonly accepted approach, found that the charged burglary and the uncharged murders were "closely related." All occurred during a short period of time on the same day in the same basic location. The victims of the murders were also victims of the burglary. Cobb committed one of the murders in furtherance of the robbery, the other to cover up the crimes. The police, when questioning Cobb, knew that he already had a lawyer representing him on the burglary charges and had demonstrated their belief that this lawyer also represented Cobb in respect to the murders by asking his permission to question Cobb about the murders on previous occasions. The relatedness of the crimes is well illustrated by the impossibility of questioning Cobb about the murders without eliciting admissions about the burglary.... Nor, in my view, did Cobb waive his right to counsel.... These considerations are sufficient. The police officers ought to have spoken to Cobb's counsel before questioning Cobb. I would affirm the decision of the Texas court.

...[*]

Page 437

233. The Court considered the effect of § 3501 in Dickerson v. United States, 530 U.S. 428 (2000) (7–2). It held that "*Miranda* announced a constitutional rule that Congress may not supersede legislatively." 530 U.S. at 444. Observing that the *Miranda* warnings "have become part of our national culture," id. at 430, the Court added that it would not overrule *Miranda* itself.

The effect of *Dickerson* on the exclusion of evidence obtained indirectly by a *Miranda* violation (see Casebook, p. 489, Note 268) is discussed at

[*] Justice Kennedy wrote a concurring opinion, which Justice Scalia and Justice Thomas joined.

length and decisions in other circuits are reviewed, in United States v. Patane, 304 F.3d 1013 (10th Cir.2002) (evidence excluded).

Page 438

236. *Elstad* is distinguished in United States v. Orso, 234 F.3d 436 (9th Cir.2000). Finding that postal inspector had used "deliberately improper tactics" to obtain incriminating statements prior to giving *Miranda* warnings, the court concluded that the taint of the statements' "coercive effect" had not dissipated when the defendant made post-*Miranda* statements and held that both statements should be suppressed. The en banc court of appeals reversed, over an impassioned dissent, and held that *Elstad* applies even if the first (excluded) confession was obtained by deception in deliberate violation of *Miranda*. United States v. Orso, 275 F.3d 1190 (9th Cir.2001).

Compulsory questioning by itself does not violate the privilege against compulsory self-incrimination, if the answers are never used in any criminal proceeding. "[A] violation of the constitutional *right* against self-incrimination occurs only if one has been compelled to be a witness against himself in a criminal case." Chavez v. Martinez, ___ U.S. ___, 123 S.Ct. 1994, ___ (2003) (6–3). The plaintiff, who was never charged with a crime had brought an action against the officer who questioned him, under 42 U.S.C. § 1983.

Page 447

240. 18 U.S.C. § 5033 provides that when a juvenile is taken in custody, the juvenile's parents must immediately be notified and must also be notified of his rights and the nature of the alleged offense. In United States v. Wendy, 255 F.3d 761 (9th Cir.2001), the court held that the parents must be informed that they will have an opportunity "to advise and counsel" the juvenile before interrogation.

Page 449

Davis is applied in Mueller v. Angelone, 181 F.3d 557 (4th Cir.1999) ("Do you think I need an attorney here?" not unambiguous and did not call *Edwards* into play).

Clark v. Murphy, 317 F.3d 1038 (9th Cir.2003) ("'I think I would like to talk to a lawyer,'" not "an unambiguous and unequivocal request for counsel within the meaning of *Davis*").

Page 460

United States v. Ingle, 157 F.3d 1147 (8th Cir.1998) (Moran v. Burbine applied).

In United States v. Moody, 206 F.3d 609 (6th Cir.2000), the court of appeals reluctantly following Moran v. Burbine, concluded that there is no right to counsel during pre-indictment plea negotiations.

Page 461

244. Also Massachusetts. Commonwealth v. Mavredakis, 725 N.E.2d 169 (2000).

McCauley is discussed in People v. Chapman, 743 N.E.2d 48 (Ill.2000). The court held that it does not apply unless the defendant's attorney is physically present at the police station where the defendant is interrogated; there is not an obligation to permit an attorney who calls the police station to be in contact with his client.

Page 469

A patient of a state psychiatric hospital was in custody for purposes of the *Miranda* requirements when he was interviewed intensively as a definite criminal suspect, in a secluded area reserved for police purposes, in isolation from other patients, notwithstanding that he was told that he was free to leave the interrogation area. State v. Stott, 794 A.2d 120 (N.J.2002).

The defendant, who was serving a prison sentence, was interviewed in a prison office about a crime for which he was subsequently prosecuted. Stating that the fact that an interview occurs in a prison does not necessarily make the questioning "custodial" for *Miranda* purposes, the court concluded that in all the circumstances the interview of the defendant was custodial interrogation and that *Miranda* warnings should have been given. United States v. Chamberlain, 163 F.3d 499 (8th Cir.1998).

Page 476

258. Police went to the home of the defendant, seventeen years old, late at night and waked him and said, "[W]e need to go and talk." The defendant said "Okay." He was handcuffed and taken to the police station in his underwear, and thereafter, after being given *Miranda* warnings, he was questioned. The state court held that he was not arrested until after he confessed. Citing *Dunaway* (Casebook, p. 472), the Supreme Court summarily reversed. Kaupp v. Texas, ___ U.S. ___, 123 S.Ct. 1843 (2003) (per curiam).

Page 480

Perkins. See United States v. Ingle, 157 F.3d 1147 (8th Cir.1998) (defendant made admissions to jail cellmate wearing recording device provided by FBI).

Page 481

261. United States v. Dortch, 199 F.3d 193 (5th Cir.1999) (continued detention of defendant after justification for traffic stop was eliminated was an unreasonable seizure).

Page 489

268. See supplement to page 437, paragraph 233, above.

Page 490

268. The effect of the decision in Dickerson v. United States, 530 U.S. 428 (2000), supplement to p. 437 above, is considered in United States v. Faulkingham, 295 F.3d 85 (1st Cir.2002) (other cases cited). The court concluded that although there might be cases in which the suppression of fruits of a *Miranda* violation was appropriate, it was not in this case.

Page 500

271.

United States v. Hubbell

530 U.S. 27, 120 S.Ct. 2037, 147 L.Ed.2d 24 (2000).

■ JUSTICE STEVENS delivered the opinion of the Court.

The two questions presented concern the scope of a witness' protection against compelled self-incrimination: (1) whether the Fifth Amendment privilege protects a witness from being compelled to disclose the existence of incriminating documents that the Government is unable to describe with reasonable particularity; and (2) if the witness produces such documents pursuant to a grant of immunity, whether 18 U.S.C. § 6002 prevents the Government from using them to prepare criminal charges against him.

I

This proceeding arises out of the second prosecution of respondent, Webster Hubbell, commenced by the Independent Counsel appointed in August 1994 to investigate possible violations of federal law relating to the Whitewater Development Cooperation. The first prosecution was terminated pursuant to a plea bargain. In December 1994, respondent pleaded guilty to charges of mail fraud and tax evasion arising out of his billing practices as a member of an Arkansas law firm from 1989 to 1992, and was sentenced to 21 months in prison. In the plea agreement, respondent promised to provide the Independent Counsel with "full, complete, accurate, and truthful information" about matters relating to the Whitewater investigation.

The second prosecution resulted from the Independent Counsel's attempt to determine whether respondent had violated that promise. In October 1996, while respondent was incarcerated, the Independent Counsel served him with a subpoena *duces tecum* calling for the production of 11 categories of documents before a grand jury sitting in Little Rock, Arkansas.... On November 19, he appeared before the grand jury and invoked his Fifth Amendment privilege against self-incrimination. In response to questioning by the prosecutor, respondent initially refused "to state whether there are documents within my possession, custody, or control responsive to the Subpoena." App. 62. Thereafter, the prosecutor produced an order, which had previously been obtained from the District Court pursuant to 18 U.S.C. § 6003(a), directing him to respond to the subpoena and granting him immunity "to the extent allowed by law."[4] Respondent then produced 13,120 pages of documents and records and responded to a series of questions that established that those were all of the documents in his custody or control that were responsive to the commands in the subpoena, with the exception of a few documents he claimed were shielded by the attorney-client and attorney work-product privileges.

The contents of the documents produced by respondent provided the Independent Counsel with the information that led to this second prosecution. On April 30, 1998, a grand jury in the District of Columbia returned a 10-count indictment charging respondent with various tax-related crimes and mail and wire fraud. The District Court dismissed the indictment relying, in part, on the ground that the Independent Counsel's use of the subpoenaed documents violated § 6002 because all of the evidence he would offer against respondent at trial derived either directly or indirectly from the testimonial aspects of respondent's immunized act of producing those documents.... Noting that the Independent Counsel had admitted that he was not investigating tax-related issues when he issued the subpoena, and that he had " 'learned about the unreported income and other crimes from studying the records' contents,' " the District Court characterized the subpoena as "the quintessential fishing expedition." [11 F.Supp.2d 25 (D.D.C.1998)], at 37.

The Court of Appeals vacated the judgment and remanded for further proceedings....

... [Further proceedings below are omitted.]

... [W]e granted the Independent Counsel's petition for a writ of certiorari in order to determine the precise scope of a grant of immunity with respect to the production of documents in response to a subpoena.... We now affirm.

II

It is useful to preface our analysis of the constitutional issue with a restatement of certain propositions that are not in dispute. The term "privilege against self-incrimination" is not an entirely accurate description of a person's constitutional protection against being "compelled in any criminal case to be a witness against himself."

The word "witness" in the constitutional text limits the relevant category of compelled incriminating communications to those that are

4. In re Grand Jury Proceedings, No. GJ-96-3 (E.D.Ark., Nov.14, 1996), App. 60-61.

"testimonial" in character. As Justice Holmes observed, there is a significant difference between the use of compulsion to extort communications from a defendant and compelling a person to engage in conduct that may be incriminating. Thus, even though the act may provide incriminating evidence, a criminal suspect may be compelled to put on a shirt, to provide a blood sample or handwriting exemplar, or to make a recording of his voice. The act of exhibiting such physical characteristics is not the same as a sworn communication by a witness that relates either express or implied assertions of fact or belief.... Similarly, the fact that incriminating evidence may be the byproduct of obedience to a regulatory requirement, such as filing an income tax return, maintaining required records, or reporting an accident, does not clothe such required conduct with the testimonial privilege.

More relevant to this case is the settled proposition that a person may be required to produce specific documents even though they contain incriminating assertions of fact or belief because the creation of those documents was not "compelled" within the meaning of the privilege. Our decision in Fisher v. United States, 425 U.S. 391 (1976), dealt with summonses issued by the Internal Revenue Service (IRS) seeking working papers used in the preparation of tax returns. Because the papers had been voluntarily prepared prior to the issuance of the summonses, they could not be "said to contain compelled testimonial evidence, either of the taxpayers or of anyone else." Accordingly, the taxpayer could not "avoid compliance with the subpoena merely by asserting that the item of evidence which he is required to produce contains incriminating writing, whether his own or that of someone else." Id. at 409–410.... It is clear, therefore, that respondent Hubbell could not avoid compliance with the subpoena served on him merely because the demanded documents contained incriminating evidence, whether written by others or voluntarily prepared by himself.

On the other hand, we have also made it clear that the act of producing documents in response to a subpoena may have a compelled testimonial aspect. We have held that "the act of production" itself may implicitly communicate "statements of fact." By "producing documents in compliance with a subpoena, the witness would admit that the papers existed, were in his possession or control, and were authentic."[19] Moreover, as was true in this case, when the custodian of documents responds to a subpoena, he may be compelled to take the witness stand and answer questions designed to determine whether he has produced everything demanded by the subpoena. The answers to those questions, as well as the act of production itself, may certainly communicate information about the existence, custody, and authenticity of the documents. Whether the constitutional privilege protects the answers to such questions, or protects the act of production itself, is a question that is distinct from the question whether the unprotected contents of the documents themselves are incriminating.

19. ... [Doe v. United States, 487 U.S. 201, 209 (1988).]

Finally, the phrase "in any criminal case" in the text of the Fifth Amendment might have been read to limit its coverage to compelled testimony that is used against the defendant in the trial itself. It has, however, long been settled that its protection encompasses compelled statements that lead to the discovery of incriminating evidence even though the statements themselves are not incriminating and are not introduced into evidence. Thus, a half-century ago we held that a trial judge had erroneously rejected a defendant's claim of privilege on the ground that his answer to the pending question would not itself constitute evidence of the charged offense. As we explained:

> "The privilege afforded not only extends to answers that would in themselves support a conviction under a federal criminal statute but likewise embraces those which would furnish a link in the chain of evidence needed to prosecute the claimant for a federal crime." Hoffman v. United States, 341 U.S. 479, 486 (1951).

Compelled testimony that communicates information that may "lead to incriminating evidence" is privileged even if the information itself is not inculpatory. Doe v. United States, 487 U.S. 201, 208, n.6 (1988). It is the Fifth Amendment's protection against the prosecutor's use of incriminating information derived directly or indirectly from the compelled testimony of the respondent that is of primary relevance in this case.

III

Acting pursuant to 18 U.S.C. § 6002, the District Court entered an order compelling respondent to produce "any and all documents" described in the grand jury subpoena and granting him "immunity to the extent allowed by law." App. 60–61. In Kastigar v. United States, 406 U.S. 441 (1972), we upheld the constitutionality of § 6002 because the scope of the "use and derivative-use" immunity that it provides is coextensive with the scope of the constitutional privilege against self-incrimination.

. . . [W]e stressed the importance of § 6002's "explicit proscription" of the use in any criminal case of " 'testimony or other information compelled under the order (or any information directly or indirectly derived from such testimony or other information).' " 406 U.S. at 453. We particularly emphasized the critical importance of protection against a future prosecution " 'based on knowledge and sources of information obtained from the compelled testimony.' " Id. at 454 (quoting Ullmann v. United States, 350 U.S. 422, 437 (1956)).

We also rejected the petitioners' argument that derivative-use immunity under § 6002 would not obviate the risk that the prosecutor or other law-enforcement officials may use compelled testimony to obtain leads, names of witnesses, or other information not otherwise available to support a prosecution. That argument was predicated on the incorrect assumption that the derivative-use prohibition would prove impossible to enforce. But given that the statute contains a "comprehensive safeguard" in the form of a "sweeping proscription of any use, direct or indirect, of the compelled testimony and any information derived therefrom," we concluded that a person who is prosecuted for matters related to testimony he gave under a grant of immunity does not have the burden of proving that his testimony was improperly used. Instead, we held that the statute imposes an affirmative duty on the prosecution, not merely to show that its evidence is not tainted by the prior testimony, but "to prove that the evidence it proposes to use is derived from a legitimate source wholly independent of the compelled testimony." Id., at 460. Requiring the prosecution to shoulder this burden ensures that the grant of immunity has "le[ft] the witness and the Federal Government in substantially the same position as if the witness had claimed his privilege in the absence of a grant of immunity." Id., at 458–459 (internal quotation marks and footnote omitted).

The "compelled testimony" that is relevant in this case is not to be found in the contents of the documents produced in response to the subpoena. It is, rather, the testimony inherent in the act of producing those documents. The disagreement between the parties focuses entirely on the significance of that testimonial aspect.

IV

The Government correctly emphasizes that the testimonial aspect of a response to a subpoena *duces tecum* does nothing more than establish the existence, authenticity, and custody of items that are produced. We assume that the Government is also entirely correct in its submission that it would not have to advert to respondent's act of production in order to prove the existence, authenticity, or custody of any documents that it might offer in evidence at a criminal trial; indeed, the Government disclaims any need to introduce any of the documents produced by respondent into evidence in order to prove the charges against him. It follows, according to the Government, that it has no intention of making improper "use" of respondent's compelled testimony.

The question, however, is not whether the response to the subpoena may be introduced into evidence at his criminal trial. That would surely be a prohibited "use" of the immunized act of production.... But the fact that the Government intends no such use of the act of production leaves open the separate question whether it has already made "derivative use" of the testimonial aspect of that act in obtaining the indictment against respondent and in preparing its case for trial. It clearly has.

It is apparent from the text of the subpoena itself that the prosecutor needed respondent's assistance both to identify potential sources of information and to produce those sources.... Given the breadth of the description of the 11 categories of documents called for by the subpoena, the collection and production of the materials demanded was tantamount to answering a series of interrogatories asking a witness to disclose the existence and location of particular documents fitting certain broad descriptions. The assembly of literally hundreds of pages of material in response to a request for "any and all documents reflecting, referring, or relating to any direct or indirect sources of money or other things of value received by or provided to" an individual or members of his family during a 3-year period ... is the functional equivalent of the preparation of an answer to either a detailed written interrogatory or a series of oral questions at a discovery deposition. Entirely apart from the contents of the 13,120 pages of materials that respondent produced in this case, it is undeniable that providing a catalog of existing documents fitting within any of the 11 broadly worded subpoena categories could provide a prosecutor with a "lead to incriminating evidence," or "a link in the chain of evidence needed to prosecute."

Indeed, the record makes it clear that that is what happened in this case. The documents were produced before a grand jury sitting in the Eastern District of Arkansas in aid of the Independent Counsel's attempt to determine whether respondent had violated a commitment in his first plea agreement. The use of those sources of information eventually led to the return of an indictment by a grand jury sitting in the District of Columbia for offenses that apparently are unrelated to that plea agreement. What the District Court characterized as a "fishing expedition" did produce a fish, but not the one that the Independent Counsel expected to hook. It is abundantly clear that the testimonial aspect of respondent's act of producing subpoenaed documents was the first step in a chain of evidence that led to this prosecution. The documents did not magically appear in the prosecutor's office like "manna from heaven." They arrived there only after respondent asserted his constitutional privilege, received a grant of immunity, and—under the compulsion of the District Court's order—took the mental and physical steps necessary to provide the prosecutor with an accurate inventory of the many sources of potentially incriminating evidence sought by the subpoena. It was only through respondent's truthful reply to the subpoena that the Government received the incriminating documents of which it made "substantial use ... in the investigation that led to the indictment." Brief for United States 3.

For these reasons, we cannot accept the Government's submission that respondent's immunity did not preclude its derivative use of the produced documents because its "possession of the documents [was] the fruit *only* of a simple physical act—the act of producing the documents." Id., at 29. It was unquestionably necessary for respondent to make extensive use of "the contents of his own mind" in identifying the hundreds of documents responsive to the requests in the subpoena. See Curcio v. United States, 354 U.S. 118, 128 (1957).... The assembly of those documents was like telling an inquisitor the combination to a wall safe, not like being forced to surrender the key to a strongbox.... The Government's anemic view of respondent's act of production as a mere physical act that is principally non-testimonial in character and can be entirely divorced from its "implicit" testimonial aspect so as to constitute a "legitimate, wholly independent source" (as required by *Kastigar*) for the documents produced simply fails to account for these realities.

In sum, we have no doubt that the constitutional privilege against self-incrimination protects the target of a grand jury investigation from being compelled to answer questions designed to elicit information about the existence of sources of potentially incriminating evidence. That constitutional privilege has the same application to the testimonial aspect of a response to a subpoena seeking discovery of those sources.... [T]he Government has argued that the communicative aspect of respondent's act of producing ordinary business records is insufficiently "testimonial" to support a claim of privilege because the existence and possession of such records by any businessman is a "foregone conclusion" under our decision in Fisher v. United States, 425 U.S., at 411. This argument both misreads *Fisher* and ignores our subsequent decision in United States v. Doe, 465 U.S. 605 (1984).

As noted in Part II, supra, *Fisher* involved summonses seeking production of working papers prepared by the taxpayers' accountants that the IRS knew were in the possession of the taxpayers' attorneys. 425 U.S., at 394. In rejecting the taxpayers' claim that these documents were protected by the Fifth Amendment privilege, we stated:

> "It is doubtful that implicitly admitting the existence and possession of the papers rises to the level of testimony within the protection of the Fifth Amendment. The papers belong to the *accountant*, were prepared by him, and are the kind usually prepared by an accountant working on the tax returns of his client. Surely the Government is in no way relying on the 'truthtelling' of the *taxpayer* to prove the existence of or his access to the documents.... The existence and location of the papers are a foregone conclusion and the taxpayer adds little or nothing to the sum total of the Government's information by conceding that he in fact has the papers." Id., at 411 (emphases added).

Whatever the scope of this "foregone conclusion" rationale, the facts of this case plainly fall outside of it. While in *Fisher* the Government already knew that the documents were in the attorneys' possession and could independently confirm their existence and authenticity through the accountants who created them, here the Government has not shown that it had any prior knowledge of either the existence or the whereabouts of the 13,120 pages of documents ultimately produced by respondent. The Government cannot cure this deficiency through the overbroad argument that a businessman such as respondent will always possess general business and tax records that fall within the broad categories described in this subpoena. The *Doe* subpoenas also sought several broad categories of general business records, yet we upheld the District Court's finding that the act of producing those records would involve testimonial self-incrimination....

Given our conclusion that respondent's act of production had a testimonial aspect, at least with respect to the existence and location of the documents sought by the Government's subpoena, respondent could not be compelled to produce those documents without first receiving a grant of immunity under § 6003. As we construed § 6002 in *Kastigar*, such immunity is co-extensive with the constitutional privilege. *Kastigar* requires that respondent's motion to dismiss the indictment on immunity grounds be granted unless the Government proves that the evidence it used in obtaining the indictment and proposed to use at trial was derived from legitimate sources "wholly independent" of the testimonial aspect of respondent's immunized conduct in assembling and producing the documents described in the subpoena. The Government, however, does not claim that it could make such a showing. Rather, it contends that its prosecution of respondent must be considered proper unless someone—presumably respondent—shows that "there is some substantial relation between the compelled testimonial communications implicit in the act of production (as opposed to the act of production standing alone) and some aspect of the information used in the investigation or the evidence presented at trial." Brief for United States 9. We could not accept this submission without repudiating the basis for our conclusion in *Kastigar* that the statutory guarantee of use and derivative-use immunity is as broad as the constitutional privilege itself. This we are not prepared to do.

Accordingly, the indictment against respondent must be dismissed. The judgment of the Court of Appeals is affirmed.

It is so ordered.[*]

. . . [Appendix to opinion of the Court omitted.]

Page 509

McKune v. Lile, 536 U.S. 24 (2002) (5–4). The defendant was imprisoned for rape. Several years before he was to be released, prison officials ordered him to participate in a Sex Abuse Treatment Program, which was designed to reduce the likelihood of recidivism. Part of the program required him to accept responsibility for the crime for which he was convicted and to give a history of his sexual activities, including criminal activities for which he had not been prosecuted. There was no immunity from use of the information in a subsequent criminal prosecution. The defendant refused to participate, on the ground that the requirements violated his privilege against compulsory self-incrimination. As a consequence of his refusal, he was moved to a less desirable prison unit and lost certain prison privileges. Noting the valid purpose of the SATP program and the limited nature of the penalties imposed, a majority of the Court held that the defendant's Fifth Amendment privilege had not been violated.

[*] Justice Thomas wrote a concurring opinion, which Justice Scalia joined. Chief Justice Rehnquist wrote a dissenting statement.

Page 519

279. Murphy v. Waterfront Commission is discussed at length in the majority and dissenting opinions in United States v. Balsys, 524 U.S. 666 (1998) (7–2). (See Casebook, p. 521.) Much of the reasoning in *Murphy* is rejected in the majority opinion.

Page 521

282. Neither a defendant's guilty plea nor her statements during the colloquy with the judge when the plea is entered constitute a waiver of her privilege against compulsory self-incrimination at sentencing. Mitchell v. United States, 526 U.S. 314 (1999).

*

PART TWO

PROSECUTION

Page 526

Rule 58. Rule 58 has been amended. Reference to a "class B misdemeanor motor vehicle offense, class C misdemeanor, or an infraction" in Rule 58(b)(2) and (3), which had been made by a 1997 amendment, is deleted and replaced by reference to a petty offense.

For the text of the rule as amended, including stylistic changes, see Appendix.

CHAPTER 7

PRELIMINARY INVESTIGATION

Page 541

United States v. Davis, 174 F.3d 941 (8th Cir.1999) (two-hour detention during which defendant made incriminating statements and after which she was released from custody, was unreasonable delay in probable cause determination, because solely for investigative purposes).

Page 542

Rule 5. Rule 5 has been amended. Rule 5(a)(1)(B) has been amended to reflect the provision of the Military Extraterritorial Jurisdiction Act, 114 Stat. 2488, that arrest warrants may be executed outside the United States. Rule 5(c)(2) has been amended to expand the options if a defendant is arrested outside the district where the crime was allegedly committed. A new provision, Rule 5(d), allows for proceedings to be conducted by video teleconferencing, if the defendant consents.

For the text of the rule as amended, including stylistic changes, see Appendix.

Page 543

Rule 5.1. Rule 5.1(a) has been amended. As amended, Rule 5.1(a) provides that the time limits provided in the rule may be extended without the consent of the defendant "on a showing that extraordinary circumstances exist and justice requires the delay." A gap in the previous rule regarding persons who are charged with a misdemeanor and consent to be tried by a magistrate judge has been filled. Other material that was previously in Rules 5 and 40 has been incorporated in the rule. The title of the rule has been changed to "Preliminary Hearing."

For the text of the rule as amended, including stylistic changes, see Appendix.

Page 546

288. See People v. Glass, 627 N.W.2d 261 (Mich.2001), overruling a prior decision, People v. Duncan, 201 N.W.2d 629 (Mich.1972), that had given already indicted defendants the right to a preliminary examination.

Page 557

Rule 44. See Appendix.

Page 558

292. An indigent defendant who has not been represented by counsel or waived his right to counsel may not receive a suspended or conditional sentence that may result in his incarceration for the underlying offense. Alabama v. Shelton, 535 U.S. 654 (2002) (5–4).

CHAPTER 8

BAIL

Page 583

§ 3142(f)(1)(A). The crime of being a felon in possession of a firearm, 18 U.S.C. § 922(g)(1), is a "crime of violence." United States v. Dillard, 214 F.3d 88 (2d Cir.2000).

Page 604

United States v. LaFontaine, 210 F.3d 125 (2d Cir.2000) (finding of danger to the community, in bail revocation hearing, upheld on basis of nonviolent witness tampering).

Page 633

United States v. Nguyen, 279 F.3d 1112 (9th Cir.2002) (forfeiture upheld).

CHAPTER 9

THE DECISION TO PROSECUTE

Page 649

312. United States v. Bass, 536 U.S. 862 (2002) (per curiam) (*Armstrong* applied; insufficient showing to justify discovery of information relating to Government's changing practice with regard to capital offenses).

Page 672

United States v. Jacobo-Zavala, 241 F.3d 1009 (8th Cir.2001) (judge's refusal to dismiss indictment at instance of prosecutor was abuse of discretion).

CHAPTER 10

INDICTMENT

Page 677

Rule 6. Rule 6 has been amended. Additional provisions for disclosure of proceedings before the grand jury have been added and a number of lesser substantive changes have been made.

For the text of the rule as amended, including stylistic changes, see Appendix.

Page 678

Rule 6(d) was amended in 1999. The amendment provided for the presence of an interpreter during deliberations of the grand jury, if necessary to assist a juror who is hearing or speech impaired.

For the text of the rule as amended, including stylistic changes, see Appendix.

Page 679

Rule 6(e)(4). An indictment is "found" for purposes of the statute of limitations when the grand jury votes to indict and the foreman signs the indictment. The fact that the indictment is then sealed is not relevant to the statute of limitations. United States v. Thompson, 287 F.3d 1244 (10th Cir.2002). The court noted that other courts have a different rule, to the effect that if an indictment is sealed *improperly*, the statute of limitations is not tolled until the indictment is unsealed. In this case, however, the court found that the indictment was not sealed in conformity with Rule 6(e)(4) and that the error was not harmless, and it ordered that the indictment be dismissed for that reason.

Page 680

Rule 6. Rule 6(f) was amended in 1999. The amendment provided for an indictment to be returned by the grand jury or by the foreperson or deputy foreperson acting in its behalf.

For the text of the rule as amended, including stylistic changes, see Appendix.

Rule 7. Rule 7 was amended in 2000. Rule 7(c)(2), pertaining to criminal forfeiture, was amended to reflect the provisions of new Rule 32.2(a). See supplement to page 1146, below.

Rule 7 has been amended. The amendment adds a reference to an exception for criminal contempt proceedings.

For the text of the rule as amended, including stylistic changes, see Appendix.

Page 681

Rule 48. See Appendix.

Page 686

329. In United States v. Sigma International, Inc., 196 F.3d 1314, 1323 (11th Cir.1999), the court found that the prosecutor's conduct before the grand jury was improper and that he had "attempted to turn [the grand jury's] ... independent decision into simply a rubber stamp decision." Concluding that his conduct did not cause the grand jury "to return an indictment that otherwise would not have issued," id. at 1324, the court concluded that the indictment need not be dismissed.

Page 691

Overruling the holding in an old case, Ex parte Bain, 121 U.S. 1 (1887), which had held that if an indictment omits an element of the offense charged, the defect deprives the court of jurisdiction, the Court held that such a defect is not "jurisdictional"; it does not deprive the court of jurisdiction to try the case and render judgment. United States v. Cotton, 535 U.S. 625 (2002). The Court went on to hold that the defect in question (failure to include facts required by *Apprendi*, see supplement to page 1108) was not plain error requiring vacation of the sentence imposed.

Page 702

337. On the duty of the prosecutor to instruct the grand jury about possible defenses to the crimes in issue, see State v. Hogan, 764 A.2d 1012 (N.J.Super.2001). The court said that such duty is related to the duty to present exculpatory evidence and is limited to defenses that would provide a complete defense to the charges. Further, the duty to instruct arises only when facts known to the prosecutor clearly indicate the appropriateness of such instructions.

CHAPTER 11

PLEAS AND PLEA BARGAINING

Page 711

Rule 10. Rule 10 has been amended. A new provision, Rule 10(b), provides for the defendant to waive his appearance for arraignment in some cases. Another new provision, Rule 10(c), allows the arraignment to be conducted by video teleconferencing, if the defendant consents.

For the text of the rule as amended, including stylistic changes, see Appendix.

Rule 11. Rule 11 was amended in 1999. There were changes of wording in Rule 11(a)(1); a new section 11(c)(6), referring to waiver of the right to appeal or collaterally to attack the conviction, was added; and Rule 11(e) was amended to distinguish clearly between plea agreements under Rules 11(e)(1)(B) and 11(e)(1)(C) and to make clear that a plea agreement may include an agreement about various sentencing factors.

Rule 11 has been amended. Rule 11(e) replaces a reference to "28 U.S.C. § 2255" with "collateral attack." Rule 11(b) replaces language tracking Federal Rule of Evidence 410 with a cross-reference to that rule.

For the text of the rule as amended, including stylistic changes, see Appendix.

Page 723

350. Rule 11(h) (Casebook, p. 714) provides a harmless error rule, comparable to Rule 52(a) (Casebook, p. 1203), for a variance from the procedures required by Rule 11. It does not contain a plain error rule comparable to Rule 52(b) (Casebook, p. 1203). In United States v. Vonn, 535 U.S. 55 (2002), the Court held that the plain error standard ("plain errors or defects affecting substantial rights") applies to errors in proceedings for the entry of a guilty plea to which the defendant made no objection and that a reviewing court can look to the entire record to determine whether that standard is satisfied.

United States v. Garcia-Luna, 274 F.3d 219 (5th Cir.2001) (failure to advise defendants of the nature of the charge was not harmless error).

Page 727

United States v. Teeter, 257 F.3d 14 (1st Cir.2001) (waiver of appellate rights).

Page 745

The Fifth Amendment's Due Process Clause and the Sixth Amendment's right to a jury trial do not require a prosecutor to disclose impeachment evidence regarding its witnesses or evidence relating to a potential affirmative defense before entering a binding plea agreement with the defendant. United States v. Ruiz, 536 U.S. 622 (2002).

Page 752

370. United States v. Randolph, 230 F.3d 243 (6th Cir.2000) (fundamental fairness required that defendant's plea agreement with U.S. Attorney's Office that he would not be subjected to further prosecution bar his prosecution by U.S. Attorney's Office in another district, on basis of information furnished by defendant pursuant to plea agreement).

Page 761

Rule 32(e). See Appendix

Page 764

United States v. Shaker, 279 F.3d 494 (7th Cir.2002). A motion to withdraw a plea of guilty is not subject to Rule 32(e) ("fair and just reason"), if it is made before the judge has accepted the plea. In *Shaker*, the judge had found that the requirements for a valid plea were satisfied but deferred acceptance or rejection until he had read the presentence report. The court noted a conflict among the circuits.

Page 765

Withdrawal. See supplement to page 1061, below.

CHAPTER 12

PROCEEDINGS BEFORE TRIAL

Page 772

Rule 12. Rule 12 has been amended, effective December 1, 2002, unless Congress acts to the contrary. The court is given exclusive authority to set a deadline for pretrial motions (rather than, as heretofore, providing for setting deadlines by local rule).

For the text of the rule as amended, including stylistic changes, see Appendix.

Page 778

Rule 7(f). See Appendix.

Page 782

Rule 8. See Appendix.

Page 783

Rule 13. See Appendix.

Rule 14. See Appendix.

Page 793

391. United States v. Mayfield, 189 F.3d 895 (9th Cir.1999) (inconsistent defenses; denial of severance was error, *Zafiro* distinguished).

Page 800

393. See United States v. Perez, 280 F.3d 318 (3d Cir.2002), in which the court discusses when the matter of venue is an issue of material fact requiring an instruction and submission to the jury. Noting a conflict among the circuits and disagreeing with the Tenth Circuit in *Miller*, the court concluded that if there is no facial defect in the indictment, failure to instruct on venue is reviewable error only if the defendant objects to venue no later than the close of the prosecution's case in chief, there is a genuine issue of material fact regarding venue, and the defendant timely requests a jury instruction.

Rule 18. See Appendix.

Rule 20. See Appendix.

Page 801

Rule 21. See Appendix.

Page 802

Rule 22. Rule 22 has been abrogated. The substance of the rule is now located in Rule 21(d).

394. United States v. Rodriguez-Moreno, 526 U.S. 275 (1999) (7–2) (*locus delicti* of carrying firearm during a crime of violence is any place where crime occurred, even if firearm was not carried in that place).

Page 831

405. United States v. McMutuary, 176 F.3d 959 (7th Cir.1999) (five-year delay during which witness became unavailable; witness's testimony merely cumulative, no violation of due process).

Rule 48(b). See Appendix.

Page 839

406. United States v. Barnes, 159 F.3d 4 (1st Cir.1998).

Page 846

408. United States v. Nguyen, 262 F.3d 998 (9th Cir.2001) (denial of continuance to permit defendant to obtain new counsel was abuse of discretion).

Page 848

Rule 16. Rule 16 has been amended. As amended, the rule broadens the defendant's duty to disclose reports of examinations and tests by substituting the word "use" for "introduce" in Rule 16(b)(i)(B).

For the text of the rule as amended, including stylistic changes, see Appendix.

Page 864

Rule 17(c). See Appendix.

Page 871

Rule 15. See Appendix.

Page 874

Rule 12.1. See Appendix.

Page 875

Rule 12.2. Rule 12.2 has been amended. The amendments make clear that a court may order a mental examination for a defendant who indicates an intention to raise a defense of mental condition; requires a defendant to give notice of an intention to raise a defense of mental condition in a capital sentencing proceeding; provides for disclosure of the result of a mental examination in connection with a capital sentencing proceeding;

provides for disclosure of the result of a defendant's expert examination; and extends sanctions for failure to comply with the rule to the punishment phase of a capital case.

For the text of the rule as amended, including stylistic changes, see Appendix.

Page 876

Rule 12.3. See Appendix.

Page 877

Rule 12.4. A new rule, Rule 12.4, concerning disclosure of the identity of a corporate party's parent corporation and the identity of an organization that is allegedly the victim of criminal activity, has been enacted.

For the text of the rule as amended, including stylistic changes, see Appendix.

Page 892

428. Securities and Exchange Commission v. Doody, 186 F.Supp.2d 379 (S.D.N.Y.2002) (on government's motion, discovery by defendant in civil case stayed until completion of related criminal case in order to avoid premature disclosure of government's case).

429. There is a strong but rebuttable presumption that a grand subpoena takes precedence over a protective order in pending civil proceedings. Only in rare, exceptional cases, when the public interest so requires, should the protective order prevail. In re Grand Jury, 286 F.3d 153 (3d Cir.2002). The court noted a conflict among the circuits and discussed the various rules.

Page 893

Rule 41(f). See Appendix.

Page 897

Rule 17.1. See Appendix.

CHAPTER 13

TRIAL

Page 898

In Sell v. United States, 123 S.Ct. 2174 (2003)(6–3), the Court held that the involuntary administration of antipsychotic drugs to a criminal defendent in order to render him competent to stand trail is permitted "only if the treatment is medically appropriate, is substantially unlikely to have side effects that may undermine the fairness of the trial, and, taking account of less intrusive alternatives, is necessary significantly to further important governmental trial-related interests." 123 U.S. at 2177. Because the issuance of the order for the administration of antipsychotic drugs in this case did not comply with those requirements, the order was vacated and the case was remanded for further proceedings.

Rule 43. Rule 43 has been amended, effective December 1, 2002, unless Congress acts to the contrary. As amended, Rule 43(b) provides specific circumstances in which a defendant's presence is not required, including an initial appearance or arraignment by video teleconferencing (see amended Rules 5, 10).

For the text of the rule as amended, including stylistic changes, see Appendix.

Page 899

See United States v. Weston, 255 F.3d 873 (D.C.Cir.2001) (administration of medication to render defendant competent to stand trial allowed).

434. Rule 43 requires that a defendant be physically present at the imposition of sentence; allowing him to appear only by video teleconferencing does not satisfy the rule. United States v. Lawrence, 248 F.3d 300 (4th Cir.2001).

Fisher v. Roe, 263 F.3d 906 (9th Cir.2001) (readback of trial testimony during jury deliberations without the knowledge of defendants and their attorneys was denial of due process).

435. For purposes of Rule 43(b)(1), a trial begins when jury selection begins. United States v. Bradford, 237 F.3d 1306 (11th Cir.2001).

Page 908

436. United States v. Durham, 287 F.3d 1297 (11th Cir.2002) (use of stun belt to prevent defendant from attempting to escape was unjustified).

Page 910

Rule 23. See Appendix.

Concerning dismissal of a juror for "just cause" (former Rule 23(b), see amended Rule 23(b)(2)(B)), see United States v. Symington, 195 F.3d 1080 (9th Cir.1999), noted in supplement to page 1114, below.

Page 922

Rule 24. Rule 24 was amended in 1999 to permit the trial court to retain alternate jurors during deliberations, in case a regular juror should become incapacitated before a verdict is reached.

For the text of the rule as amended, including stylistic changes, see Appendix.

Page 924

448. *Ross* is followed in United States v. Martinez-Salazar, 528 U.S. 304 (2000). After the judge incorrectly denied the defendant's challenge for cause of a juror, the defendant used one of ten peremptory challenges (exercised with a codefendant) to excuse the juror. The Court said that although the defendant would have been able to exercise an additional peremptory challenge had the challenge for cause been allowed, no right to due process was denied; he exercised all the peremptory challenges that the law allowed and no juror was improperly seated.

Page 931

449. See Miller-El v. Cockrell, 537 U.S. 322 (2003) (8–1) (*Batson* claim discussed at length in context of federal petition for habeas corpus).

Page 944

460. Dyer v. Calderon, 151 F.3d 970 (9th Cir.1998) (juror's false answers to questions during voir dire warranted inference of bias; conviction reversed).

Page 970

471. The *Brady* rule is discussed in Strickler v. Greene, 527 U.S. 263 (1999) (7–2), a capital case in which the court found that the prosecution had failed to disclose exculpatory evidence but affirmed the conviction because the defendant did not establish that the undisclosed evidence was "material," i.e. that there was a "reasonable probability" that the result of the trial would have been different had the evidence not been withheld.

Crivens v. Roth, 172 F.3d 991 (7th Cir.1999) (failure to disclose criminal record of prosecution witness; conviction reversed).

Page 971

472. *Brady* as affected by *Agurs*, *Bagley*, and *Giglio* (Casebook, p. 972) is discussed in United States v. Coppa, 267 F.3d 132 (2d Cir.2001). The court held that *Brady* material need not be disclosed immediately on demand by the defendant; *Brady* is not violated so long as material is disclosed in time for its effective use at trial or a plea proceeding.

Page 978

The New York Times reported on August 11, 2000, that DNA tests that were unavailable at the time of his trial had cleared Youngblood of the crime for which he was convicted. Following the Supreme Court's decision in 1988, Youngblood's conviction was set aside by the state appellate court on state constitutional grounds; but the conviction was later reinstated by the state supreme court. He served his sentence concurrently with a sentence for an unrelated crime. He was released in 1998 but was returned to prison for failing to report a change of address as required by a sex offender law.

Page 979

482. Boss v. Pierce, 263 F.3d 734 (7th Cir.2001) (prosecutor's failure to disclose exculpatory statement by a witness was a *Brady* violation, to which defense counsel's duty of due diligence did not apply, since counsel could not reasonably be expected to know that the witness had such information).

Page 981

485. Cf. Mitchell v. United States, noted in supplement to page 1159, below.

See Portuondo v. Agard, 529 U.S. 61 (2000) (7–2), noted in supplement to page 1074, below.

Rule 17. Rule 17 has been amended. As amended, the rule recognizes the authority of a magistrate judge to hold a person in contempt for failure to comply with a subpoena.

For the text of the rule as amended, including stylistic changes, see Appendix.

Page 985

After a panel of the court held that it was a violation of a federal statute prohibiting promises of favors in return for testimony, 18 U.S.C. § 201(c)(2), for a prosecutor to promise leniency to a defendant in return for testimony against his codefendant, United States v. Singleton, 144 F.3d 1343 (10th Cir.1998), the full court of appeals reheard the case *en banc* and reversed the panel's decision. The court observed that the practice of granting leniency in return for testimony is a practice of long standing. 165 F.3d 1297 (1999). Accord, United States v. Lowery, 166 F.3d 1119 (11th Cir.1999) (cases in other circuits cited).

The Fourth Circuit has held that reliance at trial on the testimony of a paid informer does not violate 18 U.S.C. § 201(c)(2). United States v. Anty, 203 F.3d 305 (4th Cir.2000).

Page 986

489. "[D]espite a defendant's unequivocal offer to stipulate to an element of an offense, Rule 404(b) does not preclude the government from introducing evidence of other bad acts to prove that element." United States v. Crowder, 141 F.3d 1202, 1203 (D.C.Cir.1998).

United States v. Becht, 267 F.3d 767 (8th Cir.2001) (*Old Chief* applied; conviction affirmed).

Page 987

United States v. McLaughlin, 164 F.3d 1 (D.C.Cir.1998) (brief recess between cross-examination and redirect examination of defendant; Perry v. Leeke applied).

During the defendant's trial for murder, the prosecutor informed the court that a witness who had apparently been threatened by the defendant and had previously refused to testify against him was willing to do so but that she was concerned for her safety. The judge directed defense counsel not to discuss with the defendant the likelihood that the witness would testify. The court of appeals held that in view of the important countervailing interest, the direction of the judge did not infringe the defendant's right to consult with his attorney. Morgan v. Bennett, 204 F.3d 360 (2d Cir. 2000).

Page 989

See Ohler v. United States, 529 U.S. 753 (2000) (5–4) (defendant who preemptively introduces evidence of a prior conviction on direct examination, after judge has ruled *in limine* that such evidence will be admissible on cross-examination, cannot challenge the admission of the evidence on appeal).

Page 992

United States v. Edwards, 303 F.3d 606 (5th Cir.2002) (trial judge did not abuse discretion in withholding information about potential jurors' names, exact addresses, and places of employment from parties); United States v. Mansoori, 304 F.3d 635 (7th Cir.2002) (trial judge committed error in withholding information about potential and actual jurors' names, addresses, and place of employment from defendant; but error was harmless).

Page 995

494. United States v. Vavages, 151 F.3d 1185 (9th Cir.1998) (*Webb* applied to prosecutor's conduct that interfered with potential defense witness's testimony).

495. After a witness had testified favorably to the defendant, government agents spoke with him in the absence of defense counsel and told him that they did not believe his testimony, that it was inconsistent with other evidence, and that if he retook the stand and testified truthfully, he would not be prosecuted for perjury. The witness recanted his testimony and gave testimony against the defendant. The court of appeals said that it was "profoundly disturbed" by the conduct of the agents, but that in view of the absence of evidence of the agents' bad faith and the extensive evidence of guilt other than the witness's testimony, reversal was not required. The court criticized most sharply the agents' failure to notify the witness's attorney or defense counsel that they intended to interview the witness and their conducting the interview in the absence of the witness's attorney. United States v. Williams, 205 F.3d 23 (2d Cir.2000).

Page 1005

Lilly v. Virginia, 527 U.S. 116 (1999). The defendant participated with two others in robberies in the course of which a person was killed. Questioned by the police, one of the codefendants gave a statement admitting his participation in the robberies and placing responsibility for the killing on the defendant. At the defendant's trial, the codefendant was called as a witness but claimed his Fifth Amendment privilege and refused to testify. His prior statement was admitted as a declaration of an unavailable witness against penal interest. The defendant was convicted of capital murder and sentenced to death.

The Supreme Court reversed the conviction. It said that the "firmly rooted hearsay exception" to the Confrontation Clause, see *Roberts* (Casebook, p. 1005) applies only if it has been shown by experience that the admission of any evidence pursuant to the exception is compatible with the substance of the Clause. Admissions against penal interest that incriminate a codefendant, the Court said, are "inherently unreliable," 527 U.S. at 130, and do not meet the constitutional standard.

Four justices added that the particular circumstances did not give a sufficient guarantee of trustworthiness to justify an exception to the general rule. Four other Justices would have remanded for consideration of that question. All Justices concurred in remanding the case for consideration whether the error in admitting the codefendant's statement was harmless.

Ohio v. Roberts is applied in McCandless v. Vaughn, 172 F.3d 255 (3d Cir.1999). The court found that the prosecution had made insufficient effort to locate an absent witness and, therefore, that he was not constitutionally "unavailable"; use of the witness's testimony at a preliminary hearing violated the defendant's rights under the Confrontation Clause.

Page 1015

At separate successive trials of two defendants for the same murders, the prosecutor, who was the same at both trials, introduced inherently contradictory evidence, which pointed to the guilt of the defendant then on trial. Both defendants were convicted. Reversing the conviction of the first defendant to have been convicted, the court held that it was a violation of due process for the prosecutor to use "inconsistent, irreconcilable theories to secure convictions for the same offences arising out of the same event." Smith v. Groose, 205 F.3d 1045, 1049 (8th Cir.2000).

Page 1024

Rule 26.2. See Appendix.

Page 1027

Rule 26.3. See Appendix.

Page 1039

In Swidler & Berlin v. United States, 524 U.S. 399 (1998) (6–3), the Court held that the attorney-client privilege survives the death of the client. The Office of the Independent Counsel had sought notes of the client after his death, for use in a criminal investigation.

Page 1041

511. In re Original Grand Jury Investigation, 733 N.E.2d 1135 (Ohio 2000) (attorney is obligated to turn over to grand jury letter written to third person by defendant, which incriminated him).

Page 1052

518. Commonwealth v. Mitchell, 781 N.E.2d 1237 (Mass.2003).

Page 1060

Cronic. In Bell v. Cone, 535 U.S. 685 (2002) (8–1), the defendant was convicted of capital murder and sentenced to death. At the sentencing hearing, his lawyer cross-examined witnesses for the prosecution but called no witnesses and made no closing argument. On collateral attack, the defendant claimed that he was denied the effective assistance of counsel. The Sixth Circuit upheld his claim and vacated the sentence. It ruled that a showing of prejudice under *Strickland* (Casebook, p. 1063) was not necessary. Prejudice could be presumed under *Cronic* because the defendant's lawyer had "entirely fail[ed] to subject the prosecution's case to meaningful adversarial testing" (Casebook, p. 1058). The Supreme Court reversed. The performance of counsel, it said, was not a total failure of representation but was allegedly erroneous in specific respects. As such, it was subject to the cause and prejudice standard of *Strickland*, which the state court had permissibly determined was not met.

United States v. Russell, 205 F.3d 768 (5th Cir.2000) (continuation of trial during two days when defendant's counsel was absent due to illness and defendant was represented by codefendant's counsel required reversal).

Page 1061

Mickens v. Taylor, 535 U.S. 162 (2002). Applying Cuyler v. Sullivan, the Court held that in order to sustain a claim that he was denied the Sixth Amendment right to counsel, a defendant who fails to object to a conflict of interest must show that the conflict adversely affected counsel's performance at trial, notwithstanding that the conflict was one about which the trial judge knew or reasonably should have known.

Before sentencing, the defendant made a *pro se* motion to withdraw his plea of guilty, in which he alleged that his lawyer had coerced him to plead guilty. At a hearing on the motion, he alleged that the lawyer had said he would not investigate the case or file motions on his behalf and was not interested in anything except a guilty plea. Stating that he did not want to be in an "adversarial position" with his client, the lawyer declined to comment at the hearing. The motion to withdraw the plea was denied. The court of appeals held that there was an actual conflict of interest between the defendant and his lawyer at the hearing on the motion to withdraw the plea and remanded for a determination whether the conflict adversely affected the lawyer's conduct. United States v. Davis, 239 F.3d 283 (2d Cir.2001).

In United States v. Henke, 222 F.3d 633 (9th Cir.2000), the defense lawyer had participated in pretrial joint defense meetings with a codefendant who later pleaded guilty and became a government witness. The lawyer was prevented from fully cross-examining the witness because of a joint defense privilege agreement. The court held that the defense motion for a mistrial because of the lawyer's conflict of interest should have been granted.

Page 1063

534. United States v. Davis, 285 F.3d 378 (5th Cir.2002) (appointment, over defendant's objection, of counsel to present mitigating evidence at sentencing phase of capital case violated his right to represent himself).

Page 1072

Strickland is applied in [Terry] Williams v. Taylor, 529 U.S. 362 (2000) (6–3). The Court held that defense counsel's failure to introduce mitigating evidence at the defendant's capital sentencing proceeding satisfied the requirements that counsel's performance be deficient and that the defendant be prejudiced thereby.

In order to show prejudice for purposes of Strickland v. Washington, it is not necessary to show that the alleged error of counsel resulted in a *significant* increase in the sentence. Glover v. United States, 531 U.S. 198 (2001). According to the defendant's allegation, his sentence had been increased by 6–21 months, which the court of appeals had said was not significant enough to constitute prejudice.

See supplement to page 1060, above.

Chandler v. United States, 218 F.3d 1305 (11th Cir.2000) (en banc) (*Strickland* applied to capital sentencing proceeding; claim of ineffective assistance of counsel rejected).

527. Burdine v. Johnson, 262 F.3d 336 (5th Cir.2001) (en banc) (counsel slept through substantial portions of trial; defendant's right to counsel denied and prejudice presumed), cert. denied, 535 U.S. 1120 (2002).

Page 1074

531. In Roe v. Flores-Ortega, 528 U.S. 470 (2000) (6–3), the defendant pleaded guilty to murder. His attorney failed to file a notice of appeal, without the defendant's consent. The defendant was not allowed to file a notice of appeal after the time for doing so had elapsed. On habeas corpus, he alleged that counsel's failure constituted ineffective assistance of counsel. Applying *Strickland*, the Court held that failure to file a notice of appeal, when the defendant has not specifically instructed that a notice not be filed, is not ineffective assistance of counsel per se. The first question, the Court said, is whether counsel consulted with the defendant about an appeal. If so, it is ineffective assistance not to follow the defendant's instructions. If not, the question is whether failure to consult is itself ineffective assistance. Such failure is not, as a constitutional matter, necessarily unreasonable and deficient. There is such a constitutional duty if a reasonable defendant would want to appeal, or if the particular defendant has indicated a desire to appeal.

In order to show prejudice under *Strickland*, the Court said, the defendant must show that but for counsel's failure, he would have appealed. This is done by showing that there are nonfrivolous grounds for appeal or that there are "other substantial reasons to believe that he would have appealed," 528 U.S. at 472. The case was remanded for further proceedings.

Page 1083

A defendant does not have a constitutional right to represent himself on appeal from a conviction. Martinez v. Court of Appeal of California, 528 U.S. 152 (2000). The Court found that the historical evidence on which it relied in *Faretta* was not applicable to an appeal and that the arguments in *Faretta* based on the Sixth Amendment were also not applicable, because it does not include a right to appeal. The interest in autonomy, the Court said, grounded in the Due Process Clause, is outweighed by the State's interest in the "fair and efficient administration of justice." The Court noted that a State might base a right of self-representation on its own constitution.

Page 1087

Waller is applied in Brown v. Andrews, 180 F.3d 403 (2d Cir.1999) (insufficient justification to exclude public during testimony of undercover police officer).

Page 1088

536. United States v. Brown, 218 F.3d 415 (5th Cir.2000) ("gag order" imposed by court, which barred parties, lawyers, and potential witnesses from making any public statements about case during trial was permissible, as least restrictive measure available to ensure fair trial).

Page 1089

Rule 29. See Appendix.

United States v. Baggett, 251 F.3d 1087 (6th Cir.2001) (discussing double-jeopardy effect of motion granted before or after jury returns verdict).

Rule 29.1. See Appendix.

Page 1099

540. In Portuondo v. Agard, 529 U.S. 61 (2000) (7–2), the defendant testified. In her closing argument, the prosecutor challenged his credibility and argued that he had heard the other witnesses testify and had an opportunity to tailor his testimony to theirs. The defendant claimed that the argument infringed his Fifth and Sixth Amendment rights to be present at his trial and to confront his accusers. Rejecting an analogy to Griffin v. California, 380 U.S. 609 (1965) (Casebook, p. 981), the Court held that no constitutional right was infringed. The prosecutor's argument, the Court said, treated him as no different from other witnesses, which in this context is sound.

Page 1102

Rule 30. Rule 30 has been amended. As amended, the rule allows the judge to ask for proposed jury instructions before trial.

For the text of the rule as amended, including stylistic changes, see Appendix.

Page 1108

Jones v. United States, 526 U.S. 227 (1999) (5–4) (federal carjacking statute; *Almendarez-Torres* distinguished).

Almendarez-Torres is questioned but not overuled in Apprendi v. New Jersey, 530 U.S. 466 (2000) (7–2), in which the Court applied to the States under the Due Process Clause the same rule that it indicated applied to the Federal Government in *Jones*: "Other than the fact of a prior conviction, any fact that increases the penalty for a crime beyond the prescribed statutory maximum must be submitted to a jury, and proved beyond a reasonable doubt." 530 U.S. at 490.

In Harris v. United States, 536 U.S. 545 (2002) (5–4), the Court considered whether *Apprendi* is consistent with its earlier decision in McMillan v. Pennsylvania. Four Justices concluded that the two cases are consistent. *Apprendi* holds that a fact that extends the maximum sentence that may be imposed must be found by a jury. *McMillan*, on the other hand, holds that a fact that increases the minimum sentence, which remains within the maximum sentence, need not be found by a jury. "Read together, *McMillan* and *Apprendi* mean that those facts setting the outer limits of a sentence, and of the judicial power to impose it, are the elements of the crime for the purposes of the constitutional analysis. Within the range authorized by the jury's verdict, however, the political system may channel judicial discretion—and rely upon judicial expertise—by requiring defendants to serve minimum terms after judges make certain factual findings." 536 U.S. at 567. A fifth Justice (Justice Breyer), expressing his disapproval of *Apprendi* generally and its application to mandatory minimum sentences in particular, concurred.

Page 1111

548. Rule 31(c), see Appendix.

Carter v. United States, 530 U.S. 255 (2000) (5–4) (*Schmuck* applied; larceny-like offense found not to be lesser included offense of robbery-like offense under 18 U.S.C. § 2113).

Page 1113

549. Smalls v. Batista, 191 F.3d 272 (2d Cir.1999) (unduly coercive charge; conviction overturned).

Rule 31. Rule 31(e) was abrogated in 2000. Criminal forfeitures are now covered by Rule 32.2. See supplement to page 1146, below.

Rule 31 has been amended. As amended, the rule makes clear that a jury can return a partial verdict, with respect to multiple counts as well as multiple defendants.

For the text of the rule as amended, including stylistic changes, see Appendix.

550. See United States v. Symington, 195 F.3d 1080 (9th Cir.1999). On the eighth day of deliberations, the jury sent a note to the judge complaining about the conduct of a juror. After discussing the matter with counsel and questioning each of the jurors, the judge dismissed the juror who, he concluded, was " 'either unwilling or unable to deliberate with her colleagues.' " The jury subsequently convicted the defendant. Rule 23(b) allows a judge to dismiss a juror for "just cause." Concluding that there was a "reasonable possibility" that the impetus for the juror's dismissal was her views on the merits, the court reversed the conviction.

Page 1114

550. In two cases, the Supreme Court of California discussed at length when a jury may be discharged after deliberations have begun. In People v. Cleveland, 21 P.3d 1225 (Cal.2001), the court held that the juror, who expressed the belief that the evidence was insufficient to prove the charges against the defendant, should not have been discharged. In People v. Williams, 21 P.3d 1209 (Cal.2001), the court held that the juror, who stated that he was unable to follow the judge's instructions about the law, was properly discharged.

Page 1115

552. See Richardson v. United States, 526 U.S. 813 (1999) (6–3), involving a *Schad* problem in the application of 21 U.S.C. § 848(a), which requires proof that the defendant committed a "continuing series of violations" of the drug laws. The Court held that the jury must agree not only that the defendant committed a continuing series but also that he committed each of the individual violations that make up the series.

Page 1119

554. United States v. Dutkel, 192 F.3d 893 (9th Cir.1999) (*Remmer* applied; conviction vacated).

See United States v. Corrado, 227 F.3d 528 (6th Cir.2000).

CHAPTER 15

SENTENCE AND JUDGMENT

Page 1128

Rule 33. See Appendix.

Page 1137

567. Contra, United States v. Jasin, 280 F.3d 355 (3d Cir.2002) (citing other cases and stating that it follows the majority rule, which is contrary to *Montilla-Rivera*).

Page 1139

Rule 32. Rule 32(d)(2) was amended in 2000, to provide that forfeiture proceedings are governed by Rule 32.2. See supplement to page 1146, below.

Rule 32 has been amended. Crimes under 18 U.S.C. §§ 2251–2257 (child pornography) are included in "crimes of violence or sexual abuse." A new provision requires the court to give notice of a possible departure from sentencing guidelines on a ground not identified in the presentence report. The entire rule has been reorganized.

For the text of the rule as amended, including stylistic changes, see Appendix.

Page 1144

571. Denial of a defendant's right to allocution under Rule 32(c)(3)(C) is not subject to harmless error analysis; a remand for resentencing is required. United States v. Myers, 150 F.3d 459 (5th Cir.1998). The court cited decisions in other circuits to the contrary.

United States v. Hall, 152 F.3d 381 (5th Cir.1998) (defendant has no right to make unsworn statement to sentencing jury in capital case).

United States v. Adams, 252 F.3d 276 (3d Cir.2001) (failure of judge to address defendant personally at sentencing invalidates sentence and requires resentencing).

Page 1145

A district court's failure to advise the defendant at sentencing that he has the right to appeal his sentence, as required by Federal Rule 32(c)(5), is error; but it does not entitle a defendant to collateral relief if he was aware of the right to appeal and was not prejudiced by the failure. Peguero v. United States, 526 U.S. 23 (1999).

Rule 32.1 Rule 32.1 has been amended. The rule is revised and expanded.

For the text of the rule as amended, including stylistic changes, see Appendix.

Page 1146

Rule 32.2. A new rule, Rule 32.2, dealing with criminal forfeitures, was added in 2000.

For the text of the rule, see Appendix.

Rule 34. See Appendix.

Page 1147

Rule 35. Rule 35 has been amended. As amended, the rule expands the situations in which a defendant can obtain a post-conviction reduction of sentence for his substantial assistance in the investigation or prosecution of another person.

For the text of the rule as amended, including stylistic changes, see Appendix.

Page 1159

583. United States v. Brimah, 214 F.3d 854 (7th Cir.2000) (Sentencing Guidelines do not bar introduction of illegally seized evidence at sentencing proceeding).

A sentencing judge may not draw adverse inferences from a defendant's silence about facts relating to the circumstances and details of the crime. Mitchell v. United States, 526 U.S. 314 (1999) (5–4).

The Double Jeopardy Clause does not preclude retrial of an issue in sentencing proceedings that had been resolved against the state. Monge v. California, 524 U.S. 721 (1998) (5–4). At the first sentencing proceeding, the state had alleged grounds for enhancement of the defendant's sentence but had offered insufficient evidence to prove it. The Court held that the issue could be relitigated in a subsequent proceeding. (See Casebook, p. 1227).

Page 1176

585. *Pearce* is applied in United States v. Jackson, 181 F.3d 740 (6th Cir.1999) (inadequate justification for increased sentence).

Page 1177

587. In Ewing v. California, 123 S.Ct. 1179 (2003)(5–4), the Court, applying Rummel v. Estelle, held that a sentence of 25 years to life for grand theft, under California's three-strikes law, did not violate the Cruel and Unusual Punishment Clause.

Page 1183

587. Cf. Hope v. Pelzer, 536 U.S. 730 (2002) (6–3) (prison discipline of handcuffing prisoner to hitching post in conditions that created risk of physical harm and inflicted unnecessary pain, discomfort, and humiliation violated Cruel and Unusual Punishment Clause).

Page 1187

590. The Supreme Court of Georgia has held that electrocution as a means of carrying out a sentence of death violates the cruel and unusual punishment clause of the state constitution. Dawson v. State, 554 S.E.2d 137 (2001).

Page 1189

See Weeks v. Angelone, 528 U.S. 225 (2000) (5–4) (adequacy of instructions concerning aggravating and mitigating circumstances).

See Wiggins v. Smith, noted in supplement to p. 1276, below.

See Hopkins v. Reeves, 524 U.S. 88 (1998) (8–1) (*Beck* distinguished).

Walton is overruled as inconsistent with *Apprendi*, supplement to page 1108, above. The right to a jury trial requires that any fact that increases the defendant's liability to punishment be found by a jury. Since under Arizona's capital sentencing scheme, the defendant could not be sentenced to death unless the judge found a statutory aggravating circumstance, the defendant's sentence was invalid. Ring v. Arizona, 536 U.S. 584 (2002) (7–2).

Page 1190

Ramdass v. Angelone, 530 U.S. 156 (2000) (5–4) (discussing *Simmons*).

Kelly v. South Carolina, 534 U.S. 246, 122 S.Ct. 726 (2002) (5–4) (applying *Simmons*).

Page 1191

Penry is overruled in Atkins v. Virginia, 536 U.S. 304 (2002) (6–3), in which the Court held that execution of a person who is mentally retarded violates the Cruel and Unusual Punishment Clause of the Eighth Amendment.

Page 1193

590. The Federal Death Penalty Act of 1994, 18 U.S.C. § 3591 *et seq.*, is construed in Jones v. United States, 527 U.S. 373 (1999) (5–4). The Court said, *inter alia*, that the Eighth Amendment does not require that a jury be instructed about the consequences of its failure to agree on a sentence recommendation, and it declined to exercise its supervisory power over federal courts to require such an instruction in capital cases.

CHAPTER 16

APPEAL

Page 1199

595. See Martinez v. Court of Appeal of California, 528 U.S. 152 (2000), noted in supplement to page 1083, above.

A state may constitutionally deny the appointment of counsel on appeal to a defendant who pleads guilty. Tesmer v. Granholm, 295 F.3d 536 (6th Cir.2002).

Page 1201

595. In Anders v. California, 386 U.S. 738 (1967), the Court required procedures to protect an indigent defendant from dismissal of an appeal as frivolous when it is not in fact frivolous, and it set forth an acceptable procedure. Under the *Anders* procedure, an appointed counsel can request permission to withdraw, accompanying his request with a brief referring to anything in the record that might arguably support an appeal. The brief must be furnished to the indigent and time allowed for him to raise any points he chooses. The appellate court must then examine the record and decide whether the appeal is wholly frivolous and, if it so finds, may then allow counsel to withdraw. In Smith v. Robbins, 528 U.S. 259 (2000) (5–4), the Court upheld a California procedure that differs from that described in *Anders*. The procedure requires both defendant's counsel and the appellate court to find that an appeal is frivolous. The chief difference is that counsel is not required to look for and point out any possibly nonfrivolous arguments.

Rule 4. Rule 4, Fed. R. App. P., was amended in 1998. In addition to organizational and stylistic changes, the text of what became Rule 4(b)(4) was amended to permit a court to extend the time for filing a notice of appeal for "good cause" as well as "excusable neglect," and the word "finding" replaced the word "showing" (of excusable neglect or good cause).

Rule 4 has been further amended. The following sentence has been added at the end of Rule 4(b)(5): "The filing of a motion under Federal Rule of Criminal Procedure 35(a) does not suspend the time for filing a notice of appeal from a judgment of conviction."

The complete text of Rule 4(b), incorporating the 1998 and 2002 amendments is as follows:

FEDERAL RULES OF APPELLATE PROCEDURE

Rule 4.

APPEAL AS OF RIGHT—WHEN TAKEN

. . .

(b) Appeal in a Criminal Case.

(1) Time for Filing a Notice of Appeal.

(A) In a criminal case, a defendant's notice of appeal must be filed in the district court within 10 days after the later of:

(i) the entry of either the judgment or the order being appealed; or

(ii) the filing of the government's notice of appeal.

(B) When the government is entitled to appeal, its notice of appeal must be filed in the district court within 30 days after the later of:

(i) the entry of the judgment or order being appealed; or

(ii) the filing of a notice of appeal by any defendant.

(2) Filing Before Entry of Judgment. A notice of appeal filed after the court announces a decision, sentence, or order—but before the entry of the judgment or order—is treated as filed on the date of and after the entry.

(3) Effect of a Motion on a Notice of Appeal.

(A) If a defendant timely makes any of the following motions under the Federal Rules of Criminal Procedure, the notice of appeal from a judgment of conviction must be filed within 10 days after the entry of the order disposing of the last such remaining motion, or within 10 days after the entry of the judgment of conviction, whichever period ends later. This provision applies to a timely motion:

(i) for judgment of acquittal under Rule 29;

(ii) for a new trial under Rule 33, but if based on newly discovered evidence, only if the motion is made no later than 10 days after the entry of the judgment; or

(iii) for arrest of judgment under Rule 34.

(B) A notice of appeal filed after the court announces a decision, sentence, or order—but before it disposes of any of the motions referred to in Rule 4(b)(3)(A)—becomes effective upon the later of the following:

(i) the entry of the order disposing of the last such remaining motion; or

(ii) the entry of the judgment of conviction.

(C) A valid notice of appeal is effective—without amendment—to appeal from an order disposing of any of the motions referred to in Rule 4(b)(3)(A).

(4) Motion for Extension of Time. Upon a finding of excusable neglect or good cause, the district court may—before or after the time has expired, with or without motion and notice—extend the time to file a notice of appeal for a period not to exceed 30 days from the expiration of the time otherwise prescribed by this Rule 4(b).

(5) Jurisdiction. The filing of a notice of appeal under this Rule 4(b) does not divest a district court of jurisdiction to correct a sentence under Federal Rule of Criminal Procedure 35(a), nor does the filing of a motion under 35(a) affect the validity of a notice of appeal filed before entry of the order disposing of the motion. The filing of a motion under Federal Rule of Criminal Procedure 35(a) does not suspend the time for filing a notice of appeal from a judgment of conviction.

(6) Entry Defined. A judgment or order is entered for purposes of this Rule 4(b) when it is entered on the criminal docket.

Page 1203

Rule 52. Rule 52 has been amended. In Rule 52(b), the words "or defects" have been deleted.

For the text of the rule as amended, including stylistic changes, see Appendix.

Page 1204

Olano is distinguished in United States v. Acevedo, 141 F.3d 1421 (11th Cir.1998). After a jury had deliberated for less than an hour and reached a verdict of guilty, the court realized that two alternate jurors had not been discharged. They had participated in the deliberations, and one of them was elected foreman. It then discharged the alternate jurors and instructed the jury to begin its deliberations again, as if for the first time. The jury returned a new verdict of guilty within about five minutes. The court said that an automatic mistrial was not necessary under Federal Rule 24(c) and that reversal was required only if there was a "reasonable possibility" that the violation of the rule had affected the final verdict. Concluding that there was no such possibility, the court affirmed the conviction.

Page 1209

600. Failure to instruct the jury on an element of the offense charged may be harmless error. Neder v. United States, 527 U.S. 1 (1999) (6–3). In a prosecution including a charge of fraud, the trial court did not submit to the jury the issue of the materiality of the fraudulent statements. Concluding that materiality was an element of the offenses, the Court remanded for consideration whether the error was harmless.

Page 1211

Rule 38. The heading of Rule 38(e) was changed in 2000 to reflect the adoption of Rule 32.2. The title then adopted was Notice to Victims, and Restitution.

See Appendix.

Page 1212

Rule 9. Rule 9, Fed. R. App. P., was amended in 1998. Stylistic and organizational changes were made.

The text of Rule 9, as amended is as follows:

FEDERAL RULES OF APPELLATE PROCEDURE

Rule 9.

RELEASE IN A CRIMINAL CASE

(a) Release Before Judgment of Conviction.

(1) The district court must state in writing, or orally on the record, the reasons for an order regarding the release or detention of a defendant in a criminal case. A party appealing from the order must file with the court of appeals a copy of the district court's order and the court's statement of reasons as soon as practicable after filing the notice of appeal. An appellant who questions the factual basis for the district court's order must file a transcript of the release proceedings or an explanation of why a transcript was not obtained.

(2) After reasonable notice to the appellee, the court of appeals must promptly determine the appeal on the basis of the papers, affidavits, and parts of the record that the parties present or the court requires. Unless the court so orders, briefs need not be filed.

(3) The court of appeals or one of its judges may order the defendant's release pending the disposition of the appeal.

(b) Release After Judgment of Conviction. A party entitled to do so may obtain review of a district-court order regarding release after a judgment of conviction by filing a notice of appeal from that order in the district court, or by filing a motion in the court of appeals if the party has already filed a notice of appeal from the judgment of conviction. Both the order and the review are subject to Rule 9(a). The papers filed by the party seeking review must include a copy of the judgment of conviction.

(c) Criteria for Release. The court must make its decision regarding release in accordance with the applicable provisions of 18 U.S.C. §§ 3142, 3143, and 3145(c).

CHAPTER 17

DOUBLE JEOPARDY

Page 1214

See supplement to page 1089, above.

Page 1228

610. Construing *Stroud*, *Bullington*, and *Poland* (Casebook, pp. 1225–28), the Supreme Court held that the Double Jeopardy Clause does not bar imposition of capital punishment at a second trial for murder after a defendant's successful appeal from a conviction, if at the sentencing phase of the first trial the sentencing jury was deadlocked and, as required by law, the judge imposed a life sentence. The first sentence, the Court said, does not count as an "acquittal" of capital punishment in those circumstances. Sattazahn v. Pennsylvania, 537 U.S. 101 (2003) (5–4).

Page 1229

612. *Burks* does not bar retrial for a lesser included offense after reversal of a conviction for a greater offense because of insufficient evidence of an element required for the greater but not for the lesser offense. Anderson v. Mullin, 327 F.3d 1148 (10th Cir.2003).

Page 1241

614. Johnson v. Karnes, 198 F.3d 589 (6th Cir.1999) (defense counsel improperly introduced evidence of defendant's prior acquittal on related charge; no manifest necessity); United States v. Stevens, 177 F.3d 579 (6th Cir.1999) (witness, without whom government could not convict, refused to testify; no manifest necessity); United States v. Gantley, 172 F.3d 422 (6th Cir.1999) (judge's display of anger at defendant; manifest necessity).

Page 1243

619. The defendant was convicted and sentenced on separate counts of robbery and murder. After serving 19 years in prison, the convictions were vacated and he was retried. He was convicted of robbery, but the jury was unable to agree on the count of murder. He was tried a second time and the jury was again unable to agree. Applying *Abbati*, the court ruled that the defendant could not be retried a third time. State v. Simmons, 752 A.2d 724 (N.J.Super.2000).

Page 1248

Issue preclusion does not bar a prosecution of the defendant for perjury after he is acquitted at a criminal trial, if the state establishes by clear and convincing evidence that it obtained substantial new evidence after the trial and was not negligent in failing to discover it sooner. State v. Canon, 622 N.W.2d 270 (Wis.2001).

Page 1252

627. United States v. Angleton, 314 F.3d 767 (5th Cir.2002) (successive state, federal prosecutions).

CHAPTER 18

COLLATERAL ATTACK

Page 1258

Fiore v. White, 531 U.S. 225 (2001) (per curiam). After the defendant's conviction became final, in another case, the state supreme court interpreted the statute pursuant to which he was convicted and determined that his conduct was not covered by the statute. The Supreme Court relied on In re Winship, 397 U.S. 358 (1970) (Casebook p. 1106), which requires every element of a crime to be proved beyond a reasonable doubt, to hold that the defendant's conviction violated the Due Process Clause.

Bunkley v. Florida, ___ U.S. ___, 123 S.Ct. 2020 (2003) (6–3) (*Fiore* applied).

Page 1259

In [Terry] Williams v. Taylor, 529 U.S. 362 (2000) (5–4), the Court construed 8 U.S.C. § 2254(d)(1), as amended by the AEDPA, which provides that a state prisoner cannot obtain habeas relief on a claim that was adjudicated on the merits, unless the state decision "was contrary to, or involved an unreasonable application of, clearly established Federal law, as determined by the Supreme Court of the United States." The Court said that a decision is "contrary to ... clearly established Federal law" if it is "opposite to that reached by this Court on a question of law or if the state court decides a case differently than this Court has on a set of materially indistinguishable facts." 529 U.S. at 413. A state decision involves an "unreasonable application of clearly established Federal law" if the state court "identifies the correct governing legal principle from this Court's decisions but unreasonably applies that principle to the facts." Id. at 413. The standard of reasonableness, the Court said, is an objective one. It noted that an "*unreasonable* application" is different from an "*incorrect* application." Id. at 365. The Court concluded that the defendant had satisfied both of those tests. See supplement to p. 1072, above.

Price v. Vincent, ___ U.S. ___, 123 S.Ct. 1848 (2003) (applying 28 U.S.C. § 2254(d)).

Also in [Michael Wayne] Williams v. Taylor, 529 U.S. 420 (2000), the Court construed 28 U.S.C. § 2254(e)(2), as amended by the AEDPA, which bars an evidentiary hearing on constitutional claims pursuant to an application for habeas corpus if the defendant "has failed to develop the factual basis" of his claims in state court proceedings, except under stringent conditions. The Court said that the failure in question is not established "unless there is lack of diligence, or some greater fault," attributable to the defendant or his counsel. 529 U.S. at 432. Diligence "depends on whether the prisoner made a reasonable attempt, in light of the information available at the time, to investigate and pursue claims in state court." Id. at 435. The Court concluded that the defendant had not been diligent with respect to one of his claims but that he had been diligent with respect to the other two.

Further provisions of the AEDPA, having to do with appeal from dismissal of a habeas petition on procedural grounds, are construed in Slack v. McDaniel, 529 U.S. 473 (2000) (7–2).

Washington v. Smith, 219 F.3d 620 (7th Cir.2000) (AEDPA applied to claim of ineffective assistance of counsel; claim upheld).

A person convicted in a state court must present his claims to the state supreme court in a petition for discretionary review, if that is possible, before seeking federal habeas corpus. O'Sullivan v. Boerckel, 526 U.S. 838 (1999) (6–3).

On the AEDPA statute of limitations, see Carey v. Saffold, 536 U.S. 214 (2002) (5–4), holding that the statute is tolled during the entire period during which the state's post-conviction review process is unresolved.

Page 1261

631. Horn v. Banks, 536 U.S. 266 (2002) (per curiam) (*Teague* analysis required).

Page 1276

See Strickler v. Greene, 527 U.S. 263 (1999) (7–2), noted in supplement to page 970.

The cause and prejudice standard does not apply to a failure to raise a claim of ineffective assistance of counsel on direct appeal. Massaro v. United States, ___ U.S. ___, 123 S.Ct. 1690 (2003). The Court concluded that such claims are unlikely to be made if counsel at trial and on appeal are the same and that even if they are not the same, the record on direct appeal is likely to be inadequate to consider such a claim, so that efficient administration dictated that it be considered in collateral proceedings in the district court. Accordingly a claim of ineffective assistance of counsel need not be raised on direct appeal.

A claim on habeas corpus of ineffective assistance of counsel in a capital case is upheld in Wiggins v. Smith, ___ U.S. ___, 123 S.Ct. 2527 (2003) (per curiam) (7–2). The basis of the claim was counsels' failure to investigate and present significant evidence of mitigating factors with respect to sentence.

Page 1277

634. An ineffective assistance of counsel claim, asserted as the "cause" for procedural default of another constitutional claim, can itself be procedurally defaulted. Edwards v. Carpenter, 529 U.S. 446 (2000). That is to say, if an ineffective assistance claim was not considered by a state court because of a procedural default for which there is not adequate cause, that claim may not serve as adequate cause for the procedural default of another constitutional claim.

Page 1278

636. See Lee v. Kemna, 534 U.S. 362, 122 S.Ct. 877 (2002) (6–3), in which, applying the rule that federal habeas corpus is unavailable if the decision in a state court rests on an adequate and independent state ground, the Court held that the asserted state ground—failure to make a motion for continuance in writing and in proper form—was inadequate, in the circumstances of the case.

APPENDIX

The Federal Rules of Criminal Procedure have been amended, effective December 1, 2002, unless Congress acts to the contrary. Some explicitly substantive changes have been made, which have been noted at the appropriate page in the Supplement. In addition, extensive stylistic changes have been made in all the rules. Some of the changes labeled as "stylistic" clarify ambiguities in the prior rule or otherwise modify the provisions in a manner that might be regarded as making a substantive change. The full text of all the rules included in the casebook are printed in this Appendix, in order. Readers are advised to examine the rule as amended closely to notice "stylistic" changes that may have a substantive effect.

Rule 3.

THE COMPLAINT

The complaint is a written statement of the essential facts constituting the offense charged. It must be made under oath before a magistrate judge or, if none is reasonably available, before a state or local judicial officer.

Rule 4.

ARREST WARRANT OR SUMMONS ON A COMPLAINT

(a) Issuance. If the complaint or one or more affidavits filed with the complaint establish probable cause to believe that an offense has been committed and that the defendant committed it, the judge must issue an arrest warrant to an officer authorized to execute it. At the request of an attorney for the government, the judge must issue a summons, instead of a warrant, to a person authorized to serve it. A judge may issue more than one warrant or summons on the same complaint. If a defendant fails to appear in response to a summons, a judge may, and upon request of an attorney for the government must, issue a warrant.

(b) Form.

(1) *Warrant.* A warrant must:

(A) contain the defendant's name or, if it is unknown, a name or description by which the defendant can be identified with reasonable certainty;

(B) describe the offense charged in the complaint;

(C) command that the defendant be arrested and brought without unnecessary delay before a magistrate judge or, if none is reasonably available, before a state or local judicial officer; and

(D) be signed by a judge.

(2) *Summons.* A summons must be in the same form as a warrant except that it must require the defendant to appear before a magistrate judge at a stated time and place.

(c) Execution or Service, and Return.

(1) *By Whom.* Only a marshal or other authorized officer may execute a warrant. Any person authorized to serve a summons in a federal civil action may serve a summons.

(2) *Location.* A warrant may be executed, or a summons served, within the jurisdiction of the United States or anywhere else a federal statute authorizes an arrest.

(3) *Manner.*

(A) A warrant is executed by arresting the defendant. Upon arrest, an officer possessing the warrant must show it to the defendant. If the officer does not possess the warrant, the officer must inform the defendant of the warrant's existence and of the offense charged and, at the defendant's request, must show the warrant to the defendant as soon as possible.

(B) A summons is served on an individual defendant:

(i) by delivering a copy to the defendant personally; or

(ii) by leaving a copy at the defendant's residence or usual place of abode with a person of suitable age and discretion residing at that location and by mailing a copy to the defendant's last known address.

(C) A summons is served on an organization by delivering a copy to an officer, to a managing or general agent, or to another agent appointed or legally authorized to receive service of process. A copy must also be mailed to the organization's last known address within the district or to its principal place of business elsewhere in the United States.

(4) *Return.*

(A) After executing a warrant, the officer must return it to the judge before whom the defendant is brought in accordance with Rule 5. At the request of an attorney for the government, an unexecuted warrant must be brought back to and canceled by a magistrate judge or, if none is reasonably available, by a state or local judicial officer.

(B) The person to whom a summons was delivered for service must return it on or before the return day.

(C) At the request of an attorney for the government, a judge may deliver an unexecuted warrant, an unserved summons, or a copy of the warrant or summons to the marshal or other authorized person for execution or service.

Rule 5.

INITIAL APPEARANCE

(a) In General.

(1) *Appearance Upon an Arrest.*

(A) A person making an arrest within the United States must take the defendant without unnecessary delay before a magistrate judge, or before a state or local judicial officer as Rule 5(c) provides, unless a statute provides otherwise.

(B) A person making an arrest outside the United States must take the defendant without unnecessary delay before a magistrate judge, unless a statute provides otherwise.

(2) *Exceptions.*

(A) An officer making an arrest under a warrant issued upon a complaint charging solely a violation of 18 U.S.C. § 1073 need not comply with this rule if:

(i) the person arrested is transferred without unnecessary delay to the custody of appropriate state or local authorities in the district of arrest; and

(ii) an attorney for the government moves promptly, in the district where the warrant was issued, to dismiss the complaint.

(B) If a defendant is arrested for violating probation or supervised release, Rule 32.1 applies.

(C) If a defendant is arrested for failing to appear in another district, Rule 40 applies.

(3) *Appearance Upon a Summons.* When a defendant appears in response to a summons under Rule 4, a magistrate judge must proceed under Rule 5(d) or (e), as applicable.

(b) Arrest Without a Warrant. If a defendant is arrested without a warrant, a complaint meeting Rule 4(a)'s requirement of probable cause must be promptly filed in the district where the offense was allegedly committed.

(c) Place of Initial Appearance; Transfer to Another District.

(1) *Arrest in the District Where the Offense Was Allegedly Committed.* If the defendant is arrested in the district where the offense was allegedly committed:

(A) the initial appearance must be in that district; and

(B) if a magistrate judge is not reasonably available, the initial appearance may be before a state or local judicial officer.

(2) ***Arrest in a District Other Than Where the Offense Was Allegedly Committed.*** If the defendant was arrested in a district other than where the offense was allegedly committed, the initial appearance must be:

(A) in the district of arrest; or

(B) in an adjacent district if:

(i) the appearance can occur more promptly there; or

(ii) the offense was allegedly committed there and the initial appearance will occur on the day of arrest.

(3) ***Procedures in a District Other Than Where the Offense Was Allegedly Committed.*** If the initial appearance occurs in a district other than where the offense was allegedly committed, the following procedures apply:

(A) the magistrate judge must inform the defendant about the provisions of Rule 20;

(B) if the defendant was arrested without a warrant, the district court where the offense was allegedly committed must first issue a warrant before the magistrate judge transfers the defendant to that district;

(C) the magistrate judge must conduct a preliminary hearing if required by Rule 5.1 or Rule 58(b)(2)(G);

(D) the magistrate judge must transfer the defendant to the district where the offense was allegedly committed if:

(i) the government produces the warrant, a certified copy of the warrant, a facsimile of either, or other appropriate form of either; and

(ii) the judge finds that the defendant is the same person named in the indictment, information, or warrant; and

(E) when a defendant is transferred and discharged, the clerk must promptly transmit the papers and any bail to the clerk in the district where the offense was allegedly committed.

(d) Procedure in a Felony Case.

(1) ***Advice.*** If the defendant is charged with a felony, the judge must inform the defendant of the following:

(A) the complaint against the defendant, and any affidavit filed with it;

(B) the defendant's right to retain counsel or to request that counsel be appointed if the defendant cannot obtain counsel;

(C) the circumstances, if any, under which the defendant may secure pretrial release;

(D) any right to a preliminary hearing; and

(E) the defendant's right not to make a statement, and that any statement made may be used against the defendant.

(2) ***Consulting with Counsel.*** The judge must allow the defendant reasonable opportunity to consult with counsel.

(3) ***Detention or Release.*** The judge must detain or release the defendant as provided by statute or these rules.

(4) ***Plea.*** A defendant may be asked to plead only under Rule 10.

(e) Procedure in a Misdemeanor Case. If the defendant is charged with a misdemeanor only, the judge must inform the defendant in accordance with Rule 58(b)(2).

(f) Video Teleconferencing. Video teleconferencing may be used to conduct an appearance under this rule if the defendant consents.

Rule 5.1.

PRELIMINARY HEARING

(a) In General. If a defendant is charged with an offense other than a petty offense, a magistrate judge must conduct a preliminary hearing unless:

(1) the defendant waives the hearing;

(2) the defendant is indicted;

(3) the government files an information under Rule 7(b) charging the defendant with a felony;

(4) the government files an information charging the defendant with a misdemeanor; or

(5) the defendant is charged with a misdemeanor and consents to trial before a magistrate judge.

(b) Selecting a District. A defendant arrested in a district other than where the offense was allegedly committed may elect to have the preliminary hearing conducted in the district where the prosecution is pending.

(c) Scheduling. The magistrate judge must hold the preliminary hearing within a reasonable time, but no later than 10 days after the initial appearance if the defendant is in custody and no later than 20 days if not in custody.

(d) Extending the Time. With the defendant's consent and upon a showing of good cause—taking into account the public interest in the prompt disposition of criminal cases—a magistrate judge may extend the time limits in Rule 5.1(c) one or more times. If the defendant does not consent, the magistrate judge may extend the time limits only on a showing that extraordinary circumstances exist and justice requires the delay.

(e) Hearing and Finding. At the preliminary hearing, the defendant may cross-examine adverse witnesses and may introduce evidence but may not object to evidence on the ground that it was unlawfully acquired. If the magistrate judge finds probable cause to believe an offense has been committed and the defendant committed it, the magistrate judge must promptly require the defendant to appear for further proceedings.

(f) Discharging the Defendant. If the magistrate judge finds no probable cause to believe an offense has been committed or the defendant committed it, the magistrate judge must dismiss the complaint and discharge the defendant. A discharge does not preclude the government from later prosecuting the defendant for the same offense.

(g) Recording the Proceedings. The preliminary hearing must be recorded by a court reporter or by a suitable recording device. A recording of the proceeding may be made available to any party upon request. A copy of the recording and a transcript may be provided to any party upon request and upon any payment required by applicable Judicial Conference regulations.

(h) Producing a Statement.

(1) *In General.* Rule 26.2(a)–(d) and (f) applies at any hearing under this rule, unless the magistrate judge for good cause rules otherwise in a particular case.

(2) *Sanctions for Not Producing a Statement.* If a party disobeys a Rule 26.2 order to deliver a statement to the moving party, the magistrate judge must not consider the testimony of a witness whose statement is withheld.

Rule 6.

THE GRAND JURY

(a) Summoning a Grand Jury.

(1) *In General.* When the public interest so requires, the court must order that one or more grand juries be summoned. A grand jury must have 16 to 23 members, and the court must order that enough legally qualified persons be summoned to meet this requirement.

(2) *Alternate Jurors.* When a grand jury is selected, the court may also select alternate jurors. Alternate jurors must have the same qualifications and be selected in the same manner as any other juror.

Alternate jurors replace jurors in the same sequence in which the alternates were selected. An alternate juror who replaces a juror is subject to the same challenges, takes the same oath, and has the same authority as the other jurors.

(b) Objection to the Grand Jury or to a Grand Juror.

(1) ***Challenges.*** Either the government or a defendant may challenge the grand jury on the ground that it was not lawfully drawn, summoned, or selected, and may challenge an individual juror on the ground that the juror is not legally qualified.

(2) ***Motion to Dismiss an Indictment.*** A party may move to dismiss the indictment based on an objection to the grand jury or on an individual juror's lack of legal qualification, unless the court has previously ruled on the same objection under Rule 6(b)(1). The motion to dismiss is governed by 28 U.S.C. § 1867(e). The court must not dismiss the indictment on the ground that a grand juror was not legally qualified if the record shows that at least 12 qualified jurors concurred in the indictment.

(c) Foreperson and Deputy Foreperson. The court will appoint one juror as the foreperson and another as the deputy foreperson. In the foreperson's absence, the deputy foreperson will act as the foreperson. The foreperson may administer oaths and affirmations and will sign all indictments. The foreperson—or another juror designated by the foreperson—will record the number of jurors concurring in every indictment and will file the record with the clerk, but the record may not be made public unless the court so orders.

(d) Who May Be Present.

(1) ***While the Grand Jury Is in Session.*** The following persons may be present while the grand jury is in session: attorneys for the government, the witness being questioned, interpreters when needed, and a court reporter or an operator of a recording device.

(2) ***During Deliberations and Voting.*** No person other than the jurors, and any interpreter needed to assist a hearing-impaired or speech-impaired juror, may be present while the grand jury is deliberating or voting.

(e) Recording and Disclosing the Proceedings.

(1) ***Recording the Proceedings.*** Except while the grand jury is deliberating or voting, all proceedings must be recorded by a court reporter or by a suitable recording device. But the validity of a prosecution is not affected by the unintentional failure to make a recording. Unless the court orders otherwise, an attorney for the government will retain control of the recording, the reporter's notes, and any transcript prepared from those notes.

(2) *Secrecy.*

(A) No obligation of secrecy may be imposed on any person except in accordance with Rule 6(e)(2)(B).

(B) Unless these rules provide otherwise, the following persons must not disclose a matter occurring before the grand jury:

(i) a grand juror;

(ii) an interpreter;

(iii) a court reporter;

(iv) an operator of a recording device;

(v) a person who transcribes recorded testimony;

(vi) an attorney for the government; or

(vii) a person to whom disclosure is made under Rule 6(e)(3)(A)(ii) or (iii).

(3) *Exceptions.*

(A) Disclosure of a grand-jury matter—other than the grand jury's deliberations or any grand juror's vote—may be made to:

(i) an attorney for the government for use in performing that attorney's duty;

(ii) any government personnel—including those of a state or state subdivision or of an Indian tribe—that an attorney for the government considers necessary to assist in performing that attorney's duty to enforce federal criminal law; or

(iii) a person authorized by 18 U.S.C. § 3322.

(B) A person to whom information is disclosed under Rule 6(e)(3)(A)(ii) may use that information only to assist an attorney for the government in performing that attorney's duty to enforce federal criminal law. An attorney for the government must promptly provide the court that impaneled the grand jury with the names of all persons to whom a disclosure has been made, and must certify that the attorney has advised those persons of their obligation of secrecy under this rule.

(C) An attorney for the government may disclose any grand-jury matter to another federal grand jury.

(D) An attorney for the government may disclose any grand-jury matter involving foreign intelligence, counterintelligence (as defined in 50 U.S.C. § 401a), or foreign intelligence information (as defined in Rule 6(e)(3)(D)(iii)) to any federal law enforcement, intelligence, protective, immigration, national defense, or national security official to assist the official receiving the information in the performance of that official's duties.

(i) Any federal official who receives information under Rule 6(e)(3)(D) may use the information only as necessary in the conduct of that person's official duties subject to any limitations on the unauthorized disclosure of such information.

(ii) Within a reasonable time after disclosure is made under Rule 6(e)(3)(D), an attorney for the government must file, under seal, a notice with the court in the district where the grand jury convened stating that such information was disclosed and the departments, agencies, or entities to which the disclosure was made.

(iii) As used in Rule 6(e)(3)(D), the term "foreign intelligence information" means:

(a) information, whether or not it concerns a United States person, that relates to the ability of the United States to protect against—

- actual or potential attack or other grave hostile acts of a foreign power or its agent;
- sabotage or international terrorism by a foreign power or its agent; or
- clandestine intelligence activities by an intelligence service or network of a foreign power or by its agent; or

(b) information, whether or not it concerns a United States person, with respect to a foreign power or foreign territory that relates to—

- the national defense or the security of the United States; or
- the conduct of the foreign affairs of the United States.

(E) The court may authorize disclosure—at a time, in a manner, and subject to any other conditions that it directs—of a grand-jury matter:

(i) preliminarily to or in connection with a judicial proceeding;

(ii) at the request of a defendant who shows that a ground may exist to dismiss the indictment because of a matter that occurred before the grand jury;

(iii) at the request of the government if it shows that the matter may disclose a violation of state or Indian tribal criminal law, as long as the disclosure is to an appropriate state, state-subdivision, or Indian tribal official for the purpose of enforcing that law; or

(iv) at the request of the government if it shows that the matter may disclose a violation of military criminal law under the Uniform Code of Military Justice, as long as the disclosure is to an appropriate military official for the purpose of enforcing that law.

(F) A petition to disclose a grand-jury matter under Rule 6(e)(3)(E)(i) must be filed in the district where the grand jury convened. Unless the hearing is ex parte—as it may be when the government is the petitioner—the petitioner must serve the petition on, and the court must afford a reasonable opportunity to appear and be heard to:

(i) an attorney for the government;

(ii) the parties to the judicial proceeding; and

(iii) any other person whom the court may designate.

(G) If the petition to disclose arises out of a judicial proceeding in another district, the petitioned court must transfer the petition to the other court unless the petitioned court can reasonably determine whether disclosure is proper. If the petitioned court decides to transfer, it must send to the transferee court the material sought to be disclosed, if feasible, and a written evaluation of the need for continued grand-jury secrecy. The transferee court must afford those persons identified in Rule 6(e)(3)(F) a reasonable opportunity to appear and be heard.

(4) ***Sealed Indictment.*** The magistrate judge to whom an indictment is returned may direct that the indictment be kept secret until the defendant is in custody or has been released pending trial. The clerk must then seal the indictment, and no person may disclose the indictment's existence except as necessary to issue or execute a warrant or summons.

(5) ***Closed Hearing.*** Subject to any right to an open hearing in a contempt proceeding, the court must close any hearing to the extent necessary to prevent disclosure of a matter occurring before a grand jury.

(6) ***Sealed Records.*** Records, orders, and subpoenas relating to grand-jury proceedings must be kept under seal to the extent and as long as necessary to prevent the unauthorized disclosure of a matter occurring before a grand jury.

(7) ***Contempt.*** A knowing violation of Rule 6 may be punished as a contempt of court.

(f) Indictment and Return. A grand jury may indict only if at least 12 jurors concur. The grand jury—or its foreperson or deputy foreperson—must return the indictment to a magistrate judge in open court. If a complaint or information is pending against the defendant and 12 jurors do not concur in the indictment, the foreperson must promptly and in writing report the lack of concurrence to the magistrate judge.

(g) Discharging the Grand Jury. A grand jury must serve until the court discharges it, but it may serve more than 18 months only if the court, having determined that an extension is in the public interest, extends the grand jury's service. An extension may be granted for no more than 6 months, except as otherwise provided by statute.

(h) Excusing a Juror. At any time, for good cause, the court may excuse a juror either temporarily or permanently, and if permanently, the court may impanel an alternate juror in place of the excused juror.

(i) "Indian Tribe" Defined. "Indian tribe" means an Indian tribe recognized by the Secretary of the Interior on a list published in the Federal Register under 25 U.S.C. § 479a-1.

Rule 7.

THE INDICTMENT AND THE INFORMATION

(a) When Used.

(1) *Felony.* An offense (other than criminal contempt) must be prosecuted by an indictment if it is punishable:

(A) by death; or

(B) by imprisonment for more than one year.

(2) *Misdemeanor.* An offense punishable by imprisonment for one year or less may be prosecuted in accordance with Rule 58(b)(1).

(b) Waiving Indictment. An offense punishable by imprisonment for more than one year may be prosecuted by information if the defendant—in open court and after being advised of the nature of the charge and of the defendant's rights—waives prosecution by indictment.

(c) Nature and Contents.

(1) *In General.* The indictment or information must be a plain, concise, and definite written statement of the essential facts constituting the offense charged and must be signed by an attorney for the government. It need not contain a formal introduction or conclusion. A count may incorporate by reference an allegation made in another count. A count may allege that the means by which the defendant committed the offense are unknown or that the defendant committed it by one or more specified means. For each count, the indictment or information must give the official or customary citation of the statute, rule, regulation, or other provision of law that the defendant is alleged to have violated.

(2) *Criminal Forfeiture.* No judgment of forfeiture may be entered in a criminal proceeding unless the indictment or the information provides notice that the defendant has an interest in property that is subject to forfeiture in accordance with the applicable statute.

(3) *Citation Error.* Unless the defendant was misled and thereby prejudiced, neither an error in a citation nor a citation's omission is a ground to dismiss the indictment or information or to reverse a conviction.

(d) Surplusage. Upon the defendant's motion, the court may strike surplusage from the indictment or information.

(e) Amending an Information. Unless an additional or different offense is charged or a substantial right of the defendant is prejudiced, the court may permit an information to be amended at any time before the verdict or finding.

(f) Bill of Particulars. The court may direct the government to file a bill of particulars. The defendant may move for a bill of particulars before or within 10 days after arraignment or at a later time if the court permits. The government may amend a bill of particulars subject to such conditions as justice requires.

Rule 8.

JOINDER OF OFFENSES OR DEFENDANTS

(a) Joinder of Offenses. The indictment or information may charge a defendant in separate counts with 2 or more offenses if the offenses charged—whether felonies or misdemeanors or both—are of the same or similar character, or are based on the same act or transaction, or are connected with or constitute parts of a common scheme or plan.

(b) Joinder of Defendants. The indictment or information may charge 2 or more defendants if they are alleged to have participated in the same act or transaction, or in the same series of acts or transactions, constituting an offense or offenses. The defendants may be charged in one or more counts together or separately. All defendants need not be charged in each count.

Rule 10.

ARRAIGNMENT

(a) In General. An arraignment must be conducted in open court and must consist of:

(1) ensuring that the defendant has a copy of the indictment or information;

(2) reading the indictment or information to the defendant or stating to the defendant the substance of the charge; and then

(3) asking the defendant to plead to the indictment or information.

(b) Waiving Appearance. A defendant need not be present for the arraignment if:

(1) the defendant has been charged by indictment or misdemeanor information;

(2) the defendant, in a written waiver signed by both the defendant and defense counsel, has waived appearance and has affirmed that the defendant received a copy of the indictment or information and that the plea is not guilty; and

(3) the court accepts the waiver.

(c) Video Teleconferencing. Video teleconferencing may be used to arraign a defendant if the defendant consents.

Rule 11.

PLEAS

(a) Entering a Plea.

(1) ***In General.*** A defendant may plead not guilty, guilty, or (with the court's consent) nolo contendere.

(2) ***Conditional Plea.*** With the consent of the court and the government, a defendant may enter a conditional plea of guilty or nolo contendere, reserving in writing the right to have an appellate court review an adverse determination of a specified pretrial motion. A defendant who prevails on appeal may then withdraw the plea.

(3) ***Nolo Contendere Plea.*** Before accepting a plea of nolo contendere, the court must consider the parties' views and the public interest in the effective administration of justice.

(4) ***Failure to Enter a Plea.*** If a defendant refuses to enter a plea or if a defendant organization fails to appear, the court must enter a plea of not guilty.

(b) Considering and Accepting a Guilty or Nolo Contendere Plea.

(1) ***Advising and Questioning the Defendant.*** Before the court accepts a plea of guilty or nolo contendere, the defendant may be placed under oath, and the court must address the defendant personally in open court. During this address, the court must inform the defendant of, and determine that the defendant understands, the following:

(A) the government's right, in a prosecution for perjury or false statement, to use against the defendant any statement that the defendant gives under oath;

(B) the right to plead not guilty, or having already so pleaded, to persist in that plea;

(C) the right to a jury trial;

(D) the right to be represented by counsel—and if necessary have the court appoint counsel—at trial and at every other stage of the proceeding;

(E) the right at trial to confront and cross-examine adverse witnesses, to be protected from compelled self-incrimination, to testify and present evidence, and to compel the attendance of witnesses;

(F) the defendant's waiver of these trial rights if the court accepts a plea of guilty or nolo contendere;

(G) the nature of each charge to which the defendant is pleading;

(H) any maximum possible penalty, including imprisonment, fine, and term of supervised release;

(I) any mandatory minimum penalty;

(J) any applicable forfeiture;

(K) the court's authority to order restitution;

(L) the court's obligation to impose a special assessment;

(M) the court's obligation to apply the Sentencing Guidelines, and the court's discretion to depart from those guidelines under some circumstances; and

(N) the terms of any plea-agreement provision waiving the right to appeal or to collaterally attack the sentence.

(2) ***Ensuring That a Plea Is Voluntary.*** Before accepting a plea of guilty or nolo contendere, the court must address the defendant personally in open court and determine that the plea is voluntary and did not result from force, threats, or promises (other than promises in a plea agreement).

(3) ***Determining the Factual Basis for a Plea.*** Before entering judgment on a guilty plea, the court must determine that there is a factual basis for the plea.

(c) Plea Agreement Procedure.

(1) ***In General.*** An attorney for the government and the defendant's attorney, or the defendant when proceeding pro se, may discuss and reach a plea agreement. The court must not participate in these discussions. If the defendant pleads guilty or nolo contendere to either a charged offense or a lesser or related offense, the plea agreement may specify that an attorney for the government will:

(A) not bring, or will move to dismiss, other charges;

(B) recommend, or agree not to oppose the defendant's request, that a particular sentence or sentencing range is appropriate or that a particular provision of the Sentencing Guidelines, or policy statement, or sentencing factor does or does not apply (such a recommendation or request does not bind the court); or

(C) agree that a specific sentence or sentencing range is the appropriate disposition of the case, or that a particular provision of the Sentencing Guidelines, or policy statement, or sentencing factor does or does not apply (such a recommendation or request binds the court once the court accepts the plea agreement).

(2) ***Disclosing a Plea Agreement.*** The parties must disclose the plea agreement in open court when the plea is offered, unless the court for good cause allows the parties to disclose the plea agreement in camera.

(3) ***Judicial Consideration of a Plea Agreement.***

(A) To the extent the plea agreement is of the type specified in Rule 11(c)(1)(A) or (C), the court may accept the agreement, reject it, or defer a decision until the court has reviewed the presentence report.

(B) To the extent the plea agreement is of the type specified in Rule 11(c)(1)(B), the court must advise the defendant that the defendant has no right to withdraw the plea if the court does not follow the recommendation or request.

(4) ***Accepting a Plea Agreement.*** If the court accepts the plea agreement, it must inform the defendant that to the extent the plea agreement is of the type specified in Rule 11(c)(1)(A) or (C), the agreed disposition will be included in the judgment.

(5) ***Rejecting a Plea Agreement.*** If the court rejects a plea agreement containing provisions of the type specified in Rule 11(c)(1)(A) or (C), the court must do the following on the record and in open court (or, for good cause, in camera):

(A) inform the parties that the court rejects the plea agreement;

(B) advise the defendant personally that the court is not required to follow the plea agreement and give the defendant an opportunity to withdraw the plea; and

(C) advise the defendant personally that if the plea is not withdrawn, the court may dispose of the case less favorably toward the defendant than the plea agreement contemplated.

(d) Withdrawing a Guilty or Nolo Contendere Plea. A defendant may withdraw a plea of guilty or nolo contendere:

(1) before the court accepts the plea, for any reason or no reason; or

(2) after the court accepts the plea, but before it imposes sentence if:

(A) the court rejects a plea agreement under Rule 11(c)(5); or

(B) the defendant can show a fair and just reason for requesting the withdrawal.

(e) Finality of a Guilty or Nolo Contendere Plea. After the court imposes sentence, the defendant may not withdraw a plea of guilty or nolo contendere, and the plea may be set aside only on direct appeal or collateral attack.

(f) Admissibility or Inadmissibility of a Plea, Plea Discussions, and Related Statements. The admissibility or inadmissibility of a plea, a plea discussion, and any related statement is governed by Federal Rule of Evidence 410.

(g) Recording the Proceedings. The proceedings during which the defendant enters a plea must be recorded by a court reporter or by a suitable recording device. If there is a guilty plea or a nolo contendere plea, the record must include the inquiries and advice to the defendant required under Rule 11(b) and (c).

(h) Harmless Error. A variance from the requirements of this rule is harmless error if it does not affect substantial rights.

Rule 12.

PLEADINGS AND PRETRIAL MOTIONS

(a) Pleadings. The pleadings in a criminal proceeding are the indictment, the information, and the pleas of not guilty, guilty, and nolo contendere.

(b) Pretrial Motions.

(1) ***In General.*** Rule 47 applies to a pretrial motion.

(2) *Motions That May Be Made Before Trial.* A party may raise by pretrial motion any defense, objection, or request that the court can determine without a trial of the general issue.

(3) *Motions That Must Be Made Before Trial.* The following must be raised before trial:

(A) a motion alleging a defect in instituting the prosecution;

(B) a motion alleging a defect in the indictment or information—but at any time while the case is pending, the court may hear a claim that the indictment or information fails to invoke the court's jurisdiction or to state an offense;

(C) a motion to suppress evidence;

(D) a Rule 14 motion to sever charges or defendants; and

(E) a Rule 16 motion for discovery.

(4) *Notice of the Government's Intent to Use Evidence.*

(A) *At the Government's Discretion.* At the arraignment or as soon afterward as practicable, the government may notify the defendant of its intent to use specified evidence at trial in order to afford the defendant an opportunity to object before trial under Rule 12(b)(3)(C).

(B) *At the Defendant's Request.* At the arraignment or as soon afterward as practicable, the defendant may, in order to have an opportunity to move to suppress evidence under Rule 12(b)(3)(C), request notice of the government's intent to use (in its evidence-in-chief at trial) any evidence that the defendant may be entitled to discover under Rule 16.

(c) Motion Deadline. The court may, at the arraignment or as soon afterward as practicable, set a deadline for the parties to make pretrial motions and may also schedule a motion hearing.

(d) Ruling on a Motion. The court must decide every pretrial motion before trial unless it finds good cause to defer a ruling. The court must not defer ruling on a pretrial motion if the deferral will adversely affect a party's right to appeal. When factual issues are involved in deciding a motion, the court must state its essential findings on the record.

(e) Waiver of a Defense, Objection, or Request. A party waives any Rule 12(b)(3) defense, objection, or request not raised by the deadline the court sets under Rule 12(c) or by any extension the court provides. For good cause, the court may grant relief from the waiver.

(f) Recording the Proceedings. All proceedings at a motion hearing, including any findings of fact and conclusions of law made orally by the court, must be recorded by a court reporter or a suitable recording device.

(g) Defendant's Continued Custody or Release Status. If the court grants a motion to dismiss based on a defect in instituting the prosecution, in the indictment, or in the information, it may order the defendant to be released or detained under 18 U.S.C. § 3142 for a specified time until a new indictment or information is filed. This rule does not affect any federal statutory period of limitations.

(h) Producing Statements at a Suppression Hearing. Rule 26.2 applies at a suppression hearing under Rule 12(b)(3)(C). At a suppression hearing, a law enforcement officer is considered a government witness.

Rule 12.1.

NOTICE OF AN ALIBI DEFENSE

(a) Government's Request for Notice and Defendant's Response.

(1) *Government's Request.* An attorney for the government may request in writing that the defendant notify an attorney for the government of any intended alibi defense. The request must state the time, date, and place of the alleged offense.

(2) *Defendant's Response.* Within 10 days after the request, or at some other time the court sets, the defendant must serve written notice on an attorney for the government of any intended alibi defense. The defendant's notice must state:

(A) each specific place where the defendant claims to have been at the time of the alleged offense; and

(B) the name, address, and telephone number of each alibi witness on whom the defendant intends to rely.

(b) Disclosing Government Witnesses.

(1) *Disclosure.* If the defendant serves a Rule 12.1(a)(2) notice, an attorney for the government must disclose in writing to the defendant or the defendant's attorney:

(A) the name, address, and telephone number of each witness the government intends to rely on to establish the defendant's presence at the scene of the alleged offense; and

(B) each government rebuttal witness to the defendant's alibi defense.

(2) *Time to Disclose.* Unless the court directs otherwise, an attorney for the government must give its Rule 12.1(b)(1) disclosure within 10 days after the defendant serves notice of an intended alibi defense under Rule 12.1(a)(2), but no later than 10 days before trial.

(c) Continuing Duty to Disclose. Both an attorney for the government and the defendant must promptly disclose in writing to the other party the name, address, and telephone number of each additional witness if:

(1) the disclosing party learns of the witness before or during trial; and

(2) the witness should have been disclosed under Rule 12.1(a) or (b) if the disclosing party had known of the witness earlier.

(d) Exceptions. For good cause, the court may grant an exception to any requirement of Rule 12.1(a)–(c).

(e) Failure to Comply. If a party fails to comply with this rule, the court may exclude the testimony of any undisclosed witness regarding the defendant's alibi. This rule does not limit the defendant's right to testify.

(f) Inadmissibility of Withdrawn Intention. Evidence of an intention to rely on an alibi defense, later withdrawn, or of a statement made in connection with that intention, is not, in any civil or criminal proceeding, admissible against the person who gave notice of the intention.

Rule 12.2.

NOTICE OF AN INSANITY DEFENSE; MENTAL EXAMINATION

(a) Notice of an Insanity Defense. A defendant who intends to assert a defense of insanity at the time of the alleged offense must so notify an attorney for the government in writing within the time provided for filing a pretrial motion, or at any later time the court sets, and file a copy of the notice with the clerk. A defendant who fails to do so cannot rely on an insanity defense. The court may, for good cause, allow the defendant to file the notice late, grant additional trial-preparation time, or make other appropriate orders.

(b) Notice of Expert Evidence of a Mental Condition. If a defendant intends to introduce expert evidence relating to a mental disease or defect or any other mental condition of the defendant bearing on either (1) the issue of guilt or (2) the issue of punishment in a capital case, the defendant must—within the time provided for filing a pretrial motion or at any later time the court sets—notify an attorney for the government in writing of this intention and file a copy of the notice with the clerk. The court may, for good cause, allow the defendant to file the notice late, grant the parties additional trial-preparation time, or make other appropriate orders.

(c) Mental Examination.

(1) *Authority to Order an Examination; Procedures.*

(A) The court may order the defendant to submit to a competency examination under 18 U.S.C. § 4241.

(B) If the defendant provides notice under Rule 12.2(a), the court must, upon the government's motion, order the defendant to be examined under 18 U.S.C. § 4242. If the defendant provides notice under Rule 12.2(b) the court may, upon the government's motion, order the defendant to be examined under procedures ordered by the court.

(2) ***Disclosing Results and Reports of Capital Sentencing Examination.*** The results and reports of any examination conducted solely under Rule 12.2 (c)(1) after notice under Rule 12.2(b)(2) must be sealed and must not be disclosed to any attorney for the government or the defendant unless the defendant is found guilty of one or more capital crimes and the defendant confirms an intent to offer during sentencing proceedings expert evidence on mental condition.

(3) ***Disclosing Results and Reports of the Defendant's Expert Examination.*** After disclosure under Rule 12.2(c)(2) of the results and reports of the government's examination, the defendant must disclose to the government the results and reports of any examination on mental condition conducted by the defendant's expert about which the defendant intends to introduce expert evidence.

(4) ***Inadmissibility of a Defendant's Statements.*** No statement made by a defendant in the course of any examination conducted under this rule (whether conducted with or without the defendant's consent), no testimony by the expert based on the statement, and no other fruits of the statement may be admitted into evidence against the defendant in any criminal proceeding except on an issue regarding mental condition on which the defendant:

(A) has introduced evidence of incompetency or evidence requiring notice under Rule 12.2(a) or (b)(1), or

(B) has introduced expert evidence in a capital sentencing proceeding requiring notice under Rule 12.2(b)(2).

(d) Failure to Comply. If the defendant fails to give notice under Rule 12.2(b) or does not submit to an examination when ordered under Rule 12.2(c), the court may exclude any expert evidence from the defendant on the issue of the defendant's mental disease, mental defect, or any other mental condition bearing on the defendant's guilt or the issue of punishment in a capital case.

(e) Inadmissibility of Withdrawn Intention. Evidence of an intention as to which notice was given under Rule 12.2(a) or (b), later withdrawn, is not, in any civil or criminal proceeding, admissible against the person who gave notice of the intention.

Rule 12.3.

NOTICE OF A PUBLIC-AUTHORITY DEFENSE

(a) Notice of the Defense and Disclosure of Witnesses.

(1) ***Notice in General.*** If a defendant intends to assert a defense of actual or believed exercise of public authority on behalf of a law enforcement agency or federal intelligence agency at the time of the alleged offense, the defendant must so notify an attorney for the government in writing and must file a copy of the notice with the clerk within the time provided for filing a pretrial motion, or at any later time the court sets. The notice filed with the clerk must be under seal if the notice identifies a federal intelligence agency as the source of public authority.

(2) *Contents of Notice.* The notice must contain the following information:

(A) the law enforcement agency or federal intelligence agency involved;

(B) the agency member on whose behalf the defendant claims to have acted; and

(C) the time during which the defendant claims to have acted with public authority.

(3) *Response to the Notice.* An attorney for the government must serve a written response on the defendant or the defendant's attorney within 10 days after receiving the defendant's notice, but no later than 20 days before trial. The response must admit or deny that the defendant exercised the public authority identified in the defendant's notice.

(4) *Disclosing Witnesses.*

(A) *Government's Request.* An attorney for the government may request in writing that the defendant disclose the name, address, and telephone number of each witness the defendant intends to rely on to establish a public-authority defense. An attorney for the government may serve the request when the government serves its response to the defendant's notice under Rule 12.3(a)(3), or later, but must serve the request no later than 20 days before trial.

(B) *Defendant's Response.* Within 7 days after receiving the government's request, the defendant must serve on an attorney for the government a written statement of the name, address, and telephone number of each witness.

(C) *Government's Reply.* Within 7 days after receiving the defendant's statement, an attorney for the government must serve on the defendant or the defendant's attorney a written statement of the name, address, and telephone number of each witness the government intends to rely on to oppose the defendant's public-authority defense.

(5) ***Additional Time.*** The court may, for good cause, allow a party additional time to comply with this rule.

(b) Continuing Duty to Disclose. Both an attorney for the government and the defendant must promptly disclose in writing to the other party the name, address, and telephone number of any additional witness if:

(1) the disclosing party learns of the witness before or during trial; and

(2) the witness should have been disclosed under Rule 12.3(a)(4) if the disclosing party had known of the witness earlier.

(c) Failure to Comply. If a party fails to comply with this rule, the court may exclude the testimony of any undisclosed witness regarding the public-authority defense. This rule does not limit the defendant's right to testify.

(d) Protective Procedures Unaffected. This rule does not limit the court's authority to issue appropriate protective orders or to order that any filings be under seal.

(e) Inadmissibility of Withdrawn Intention. Evidence of an intention as to which notice was given under Rule 12.3(a), later withdrawn, is not, in any civil or criminal proceeding, admissible against the person who gave notice of the intention.

Rule 12.4.

DISCLOSURE STATEMENT

(a) Who Must File.

(1) ***Nongovernmental Corporate Party.*** Any nongovernmental corporate party to a proceeding in a district court must file a statement that identifies any parent corporation and any publicly held corporation that owns 10% or more of its stock or states that there is no such corporation.

(2) ***Organizational Victim.*** If an organization is a victim of the alleged criminal activity, the government must file a statement identifying the victim. If the organizational victim is a corporation, the statement must also disclose the information required by Rule 12.4(a)(1) to the extent it can be obtained through due diligence.

(b) Time for Filing; Supplemental Filing. A party must:

(1) file the Rule 12.4(a) statement upon the defendant's initial appearance; and

(2) promptly file a supplemental statement upon any change in the information that the statement requires.

Rule 13.

JOINT TRIAL OF SEPARATE CASES

The court may order that separate cases be tried together as though brought in a single indictment or information if all offenses and all defendants could have been joined in a single indictment or information.

Rule 14.

RELIEF FROM PREJUDICIAL JOINDER

(a) Relief. If the joinder of offenses or defendants in an indictment, an information, or a consolidation for trial appears to prejudice a defendant or the government, the court may order separate trials of counts, sever the defendants' trials, or provide any other relief that justice requires.

(b) Defendant's Statements. Before ruling on a defendant's motion to sever, the court may order an attorney for the government to deliver to the court for in camera inspection any defendant's statement that the government intends to use as evidence.

Rule 15.

DEPOSITIONS

(a) When Taken.

(1) ***In General.*** A party may move that a prospective witness be deposed in order to preserve testimony for trial. The court may grant the motion because of exceptional circumstances and in the interest of justice. If the court orders the deposition to be taken, it may also require the deponent to produce at the deposition any designated material that is not privileged, including any book, paper, document, record, recording, or data.

(2) ***Detained Material Witness.*** A witness who is detained under 18 U.S.C. § 3144 may request to be deposed by filing a written motion and giving notice to the parties. The court may then order that the deposition be taken and may discharge the witness after the witness has signed under oath the deposition transcript.

(b) Notice.

(1) ***In General.*** A party seeking to take a deposition must give every other party reasonable written notice of the deposition's date and location. The notice must state the name and address of each deponent. If requested by a party receiving the notice, the court may, for good cause, change the deposition's date or location.

(2) ***To the Custodial Officer.*** A party seeking to take the deposition must also notify the officer who has custody of the defendant of the scheduled date and location.

(c) Defendant's Presence.

(1) ***Defendant in Custody.*** The officer who has custody of the defendant must produce the defendant at the deposition and keep the defendant in the witness's presence during the examination, unless the defendant:

(A) waives in writing the right to be present; or

(B) persists in disruptive conduct justifying exclusion after being warned by the court that disruptive conduct will result in the defendant's exclusion.

(2) ***Defendant Not in Custody.*** A defendant who is not in custody has the right upon request to be present at the deposition, subject to any conditions imposed by the court. If the government tenders the defendant's expenses as provided in Rule 15(d) but the defendant still fails to appear, the defendant—absent good cause—waives both the right to appear and any objection to the taking and use of the deposition based on that right.

(d) Expenses. If the deposition was requested by the government, the court may—or if the defendant is unable to bear the deposition expenses, the court must—order the government to pay:

(1) any reasonable travel and subsistence expenses of the defendant and the defendant's attorney to attend the deposition; and

(2) the costs of the deposition transcript.

(e) Manner of Taking. Unless these rules or a court order provides otherwise, a deposition must be taken and filed in the same manner as a deposition in a civil action, except that:

(1) A defendant may not be deposed without that defendant's consent.

(2) The scope and manner of the deposition examination and cross-examination must be the same as would be allowed during trial.

(3) The government must provide to the defendant or the defendant's attorney, for use at the deposition, any statement of the deponent in the government's possession to which the defendant would be entitled at trial.

(f) Use as Evidence. A party may use all or part of a deposition as provided by the Federal Rules of Evidence.

(g) Objections. A party objecting to deposition testimony or evidence must state the grounds for the objection during the deposition.

(h) Depositions by Agreement Permitted. The parties may by agreement take and use a deposition with the court's consent.

Rule 16.

DISCOVERY AND INSPECTION

(a) Government's Disclosure.

(1) Information Subject to Disclosure.

(A) *Defendant's Oral Statement.* Upon a defendant's request, the government must disclose to the defendant the substance of any relevant oral statement made by the defendant, before or after arrest, in response to interrogation by a person the defendant knew was a government agent if the government intends to use the statement at trial.

(B) *Defendant's Written or Recorded Statement.* Upon a defendant's request, the government must disclose to the defendant, and make available for inspection, copying, or photographing, all of the following:

(i) any relevant written or recorded statement by the defendant if:

- the statement is within the government's possession, custody, or control; and
- the attorney for the government knows—or through due diligence could know—that the statement exists;

(ii) the portion of any written record containing the substance of any relevant oral statement made before or after arrest if the defendant made the statement in response to interrogation by a person the defendant knew was a government agent; and

(iii) the defendant's recorded testimony before a grand jury relating to the charged offense.

(C) *Organizational Defendant.* Upon a defendant's request, if the defendant is an organization, the government must disclose to the defendant any statement described in Rule 16(a)(1)(A) and (B) if the government contends that the person making the statement:

(i) was legally able to bind the defendant regarding the subject of the statement because of that person's position as the defendant's director, officer, employee, or agent; or

(ii) was personally involved in the alleged conduct constituting the offense and was legally able to bind the defendant regarding that conduct because of that person's position as the defendant's director, officer, employee, or agent.

(D) *Defendant's Prior Record.* Upon a defendant's request, the government must furnish the defendant with a copy of the defendant's prior criminal record that is within the government's possession, custody, or control if the attorney for the government knows—or through due diligence could know—that the record exists.

(E) *Documents and Objects.* Upon a defendant's request, the government must permit the defendant to inspect and to copy or photograph books, papers, documents, data, photographs, tangible objects, buildings or places, or copies or portions of any of these items, if the item is within the government's possession, custody, or control and:

(i) the item is material to preparing the defense;

(ii) the government intends to use the item in its case-in-chief at trial; or

(iii) the item was obtained from or belongs to the defendant.

(F) *Reports of Examinations and Tests.* Upon a defendant's request, the government must permit a defendant to inspect and to copy or photograph the results or reports of any physical or mental examination and of any scientific test or experiment if:

(i) the item is within the government's possession, custody, or control;

(ii) the attorney for the government knows—or through due diligence could know—that the item exists; and

(iii) the item is material to preparing the defense or the government intends to use the item in its case-in-chief at trial.

(G) *Expert Testimony.* Upon a defendant's request, the government must give the defendant a written summary of any testimony the government intends to use in its case-in-chief at trial under Federal Rules of Evidence 702, 703, or 705. The summary must describe the witness's opinions, the bases and reasons for those opinions, and the witness's qualifications.

(2) *Information Not Subject to Disclosure.* Except as Rule 16(a)(1) provides otherwise, this rule does not authorize the discovery or inspection of reports, memoranda, or other internal government documents made by an attorney for the government or other government agent in connection with investigating or prosecuting the case. Nor does this rule authorize the discovery or inspection of statements made by prospective government witnesses except as provided in 18 U.S.C. § 3500.

(3) *Grand Jury Transcripts.* This rule does not apply to the discovery or inspection of a grand jury's recorded proceedings, except as provided in Rules 6, 12(h), 16(a)(1), and 26.2.

(b) Defendant's Disclosure.

(1) *Information Subject to Disclosure.*

(A) *Documents and Objects.* If a defendant requests disclosure under Rule 16(a)(1)(E) and the government complies, then the defendant must permit the government, upon request, to inspect and to copy or photograph books, papers, documents, data, photographs, tangible objects, buildings or places, or copies or portions of any of these items if:

(i) the item is within the defendant's possession, custody, or control; and

(ii) the defendant intends to use the item in the defendant's case-in-chief at trial.

(B) *Reports of Examinations and Tests.* If a defendant requests disclosure under Rule 16(a)(1)(F) and the government complies, the defendant must permit the government, upon request, to inspect and to copy or photograph the results or reports of any physical or mental examination and of any scientific test or experiment if:

(i) the item is within the defendant's possession, custody, or control; and

(ii) the defendant intends to use the item in the defendant's case-in-chief at trial, or intends to call the witness who prepared the report and the report relates to the witness's testimony.

(C) *Expert Testimony.* If a defendant requests disclosure under Rule 16(a)(1)(G) and the government complies, the defendant must give the government, upon request, a written summary of any testimony the defendant intends to use as evidence at trial under Federal Rules of Evidence 702, 703, or 705. The summary must describe the witness's opinions, the bases and reasons for these opinions, and the witness's qualifications.

(2) *Information Not Subject to Disclosure.* Except for scientific or medical reports, Rule 16(b)(1) does not authorize discovery or inspection of:

(A) reports, memoranda, or other documents made by the defendant, or the defendant's attorney or agent, during the case's investigation or defense; or

(B) a statement made to the defendant, or the defendant's attorney or agent, by:

(i) the defendant;

(ii) a government or defense witness; or

(iii) a prospective government or defense witness.

(c) Continuing Duty to Disclose. A party who discovers additional evidence or material before or during trial must promptly disclose its existence to the other party or the court if:

(1) the evidence or material is subject to discovery or inspection under this rule; and

(2) the other party previously requested, or the court ordered, its production.

(d) Regulating Discovery.

(1) ***Protective and Modifying Orders.*** At any time the court may, for good cause, deny, restrict, or defer discovery or inspection, or grant other appropriate relief. The court may permit a party to show good cause by a written statement that the court will inspect ex parte. If relief is granted, the court must preserve the entire text of the party's statement under seal.

(2) ***Failure to Comply.*** If a party fails to comply with this rule, the court may:

(A) order that party to permit the discovery or inspection; specify its time, place, and manner; and prescribe other just terms and conditions;

(B) grant a continuance;

(C) prohibit that party from introducing the undisclosed evidence; or

(D) enter any other order that is just under the circumstances.

Rule 17.

SUBPOENA

(a) Content. A subpoena must state the court's name and the title of the proceeding, include the seal of the court, and command the witness to attend and testify at the time and place the subpoena specifies. The clerk must issue a blank subpoena—signed and sealed—to the party requesting it, and that party must fill in the blanks before the subpoena is served.

(b) Defendant Unable to Pay. Upon a defendant's ex parte application, the court must order that a subpoena be issued for a named witness if the defendant shows an inability to pay the witness's fees and the necessity of the witness's presence for an adequate defense. If the court orders a subpoena to be issued, the process costs and witness fees will be paid in the same manner as those paid for witnesses the government subpoenas.

(c) Producing Documents and Objects.

(1) *In General.* A subpoena may order the witness to produce any books, papers, documents, data, or other objects the subpoena designates. The court may direct the witness to produce the designated items in court before trial or before they are to be offered in evidence. When the items arrive, the court may permit the parties and their attorneys to inspect all or part of them.

(2) *Quashing or Modifying the Subpoena.* On motion made promptly, the court may quash or modify the subpoena if compliance would be unreasonable or oppressive.

(d) Service. A marshal, a deputy marshal, or any nonparty who is at least 18 years old may serve a subpoena. The server must deliver a copy of the subpoena to the witness and must tender to the witness one day's witness-attendance fee and the legal mileage allowance. The server need not tender the attendance fee or mileage allowance when the United States, a federal officer, or a federal agency has requested the subpoena.

(e) Place of Service.

(1) *In the United States.* A subpoena requiring a witness to attend a hearing or trial may be served at any place within the United States.

(2) *In a Foreign Country.* If the witness is in a foreign country, 28 U.S.C. § 1783 governs the subpoena's service.

(f) Issuing a Deposition Subpoena.

(1) *Issuance.* A court order to take a deposition authorizes the clerk in the district where the deposition is to be taken to issue a subpoena for any witness named or described in the order.

(2) *Place.* After considering the convenience of the witness and the parties, the court may order—and the subpoena may require—the witness to appear anywhere the court designates.

(g) Contempt. The court (other than a magistrate judge) may hold in contempt a witness who, without adequate excuse, disobeys a subpoena issued by a federal court in that district. A magistrate judge may hold in contempt a witness who, without adequate excuse, disobeys a subpoena issued by that magistrate judge as provided in 28 U.S.C. § 636(e).

(h) Information Not Subject to a Subpoena. No party may subpoena a statement of a witness or of a prospective witness under this rule. Rule 26.2 governs the production of the statement.

Rule 17.1.

PRETRIAL CONFERENCE

On its own, or on a party's motion, the court may hold one or more pretrial conferences to promote a fair and expeditious trial. When a conference ends, the court must prepare and file a memorandum of any matters agreed to during the conference. The government may not use any statement made during the conference by the defendant or the defendant's attorney unless it is in writing and is signed by the defendant and the defendant's attorney.

Rule 18.

PLACE OF PROSECUTION AND TRIAL

Unless a statute or these rules permit otherwise, the government must prosecute an offense in a district where the offense was committed. The court must set the place of trial within the district with due regard for the convenience of the defendant and the witnesses, and the prompt administration of justice.

Rule 20.

TRANSFER FOR PLEA AND SENTENCE

(a) Consent to Transfer. A prosecution may be transferred from the district where the indictment or information is pending, or from which a warrant on a complaint has been issued, to the district where the defendant is arrested, held, or present if:

(1) the defendant states in writing a wish to plead guilty or nolo contendere and to waive trial in the district where the indictment, information, or complaint is pending, consents in writing to the court's disposing of the case in the transferee district, and files the statement in the transferee district; and

(2) the United States attorneys in both districts approve the transfer in writing.

(b) Clerk's Duties. After receiving the defendant's statement and the required approvals, the clerk where the indictment, information, or complaint is pending must send the file, or a certified copy, to the clerk in the transferee district.

(c) Effect of a Not Guilty Plea. If the defendant pleads not guilty after the case has been transferred under Rule 20(a), the clerk must return the papers to the court where the prosecution began, and that court must restore the proceeding to its docket. The defendant's statement that the defendant wished to plead guilty or nolo contendere is not, in any civil or criminal proceeding, admissible against the defendant.

(d) Juveniles.

(1) *Consent to Transfer.* A juvenile, as defined in 18 U.S.C. § 5031, may be proceeded against as a juvenile delinquent in the district where the juvenile is arrested, held, or present if:

(A) the alleged offense that occurred in the other district is not punishable by death or life imprisonment;

(B) an attorney has advised the juvenile;

(C) the court has informed the juvenile of the juvenile's rights—including the right to be returned to the district where the offense allegedly occurred—and the consequences of waiving those rights;

(D) the juvenile, after receiving the court's information about rights, consents in writing to be proceeded against in the transferee district, and files the consent in the transferee district;

(E) the United States attorneys for both districts approve the transfer in writing; and

(F) the transferee court approves the transfer.

(2) *Clerk's Duties.* After receiving the juvenile's written consent and the required approvals, the clerk where the indictment, information, or complaint is pending or where the alleged offense occurred must send the file, or a certified copy, to the clerk in the transferee district.

Rule 21.

TRANSFER FOR TRIAL

(a) For Prejudice. Upon the defendant's motion, the court must transfer the proceeding against that defendant to another district if the court is satisfied that so great a prejudice against the defendant exists in the transferring district that the defendant cannot obtain a fair and impartial trial there.

(b) For Convenience. Upon the defendant's motion, the court may transfer the proceeding, or one or more counts, against that defendant to another district for the convenience of the parties and witnesses and in the interest of justice.

(c) Proceedings on Transfer. When the court orders a transfer, the clerk must send to the transferee district the file, or a certified copy, and any bail taken. The prosecution will then continue in the transferee district.

(d) Time to File a Motion to Transfer. A motion to transfer may be made at or before arraignment or at any other time the court or these rules prescribe.

Rule 23.

JURY OR NONJURY TRIAL

(a) Jury Trial. If the defendant is entitled to a jury trial, the trial must be by jury unless:

(1) the defendant waives a jury trial in writing;

(2) the government consents; and

(3) the court approves.

(b) Jury Size.

(1) *In General.* A jury consists of 12 persons unless this rule provides otherwise.

(2) *Stipulation for a Smaller Jury.* At any time before the verdict, the parties may, with the court's approval, stipulate in writing that:

(A) the jury may consist of fewer than 12 persons; or

(B) a jury of fewer than 12 persons may return a verdict if the court finds it necessary to excuse a juror for good cause after the trial begins.

(3) *Court Order for a Jury of 11.* After the jury has retired to deliberate, the court may permit a jury of 11 persons to return a verdict, even without a stipulation by the parties, if the court finds good cause to excuse a juror.

(c) Nonjury Trial. In a case tried without a jury, the court must find the defendant guilty or not guilty. If a party requests before the finding of guilty or not guilty, the court must state its specific findings of fact in open court or in a written decision or opinion.

Rule 24.

TRIAL JURORS

(a) Examination.

(1) *In General.* The court may examine prospective jurors or may permit the attorneys for the parties to do so.

(2) *Court Examination.* If the court examines the jurors, it must permit the attorneys for the parties to:

(A) ask further questions that the court considers proper; or

(B) submit further questions that the court may ask if it considers them proper.

(b) Peremptory Challenges. Each side is entitled to the number of peremptory challenges to prospective jurors specified below. The court may allow additional peremptory challenges to multiple defendants, and may allow the defendants to exercise those challenges separately or jointly.

(1) *Capital Case.* Each side has 20 peremptory challenges when the government seeks the death penalty.

(2) ***Other Felony Case.*** The government has 6 peremptory challenges and the defendant or defendants jointly have 10 peremptory challenges when the defendant is charged with a crime punishable by imprisonment of more than one year.

(3) ***Misdemeanor Case.*** Each side has 3 peremptory challenges when the defendant is charged with a crime punishable by fine, imprisonment of one year or less, or both.

(c) Alternate Jurors.

(1) ***In General.*** The court may impanel up to 6 alternate jurors to replace any jurors who are unable to perform or who are disqualified from performing their duties.

(2) ***Procedure.***

(A) Alternate jurors must have the same qualifications and be selected and sworn in the same manner as any other juror.

(B) Alternate jurors replace jurors in the same sequence in which the alternates were selected. An alternate juror who replaces a juror has the same authority as the other jurors.

(3) ***Retaining Alternate Jurors.*** The court may retain alternate jurors after the jury retires to deliberate. The court must ensure that a retained alternate does not discuss the case with anyone until that alternate replaces a juror or is discharged. If an alternate replaces a juror after deliberations have begun, the court must instruct the jury to begin its deliberations anew.

(4) ***Peremptory Challenges.*** Each side is entitled to the number of additional peremptory challenges to prospective alternate jurors specified below. These additional challenges may be used only to remove alternate jurors.

(A) *One or Two Alternates.* One additional peremptory challenge is permitted when one or two alternates are impaneled.

(B) *Three or Four Alternates.* Two additional peremptory challenges are permitted when three or four alternates are impaneled.

(C) *Five or Six Alternates.* Three additional peremptory challenges are permitted when five or six alternates are impaneled.

Rule 26.2.

PRODUCING A WITNESS'S STATEMENT

(a) Motion to Produce. After a witness other than the defendant has testified on direct examination, the court, on motion of a party who did not call the witness, must order an attorney for the government or the defendant and the defendant's attorney to produce, for the examination and use of the moving party, any statement of the witness that is in their possession and that relates to the subject matter of the witness's testimony.

(b) Producing the Entire Statement. If the entire statement relates to the subject matter of the witness's testimony, the court must order that the statement be delivered to the moving party.

(c) Producing a Redacted Statement. If the party who called the witness claims that the statement contains information that is privileged or does not relate to the subject matter of the witness's testimony, the court must inspect the statement in camera. After excising any privileged or unrelated portions, the court must order delivery of the redacted statement to the moving party. If the defendant objects to an excision, the court must preserve the entire statement with the excised portion indicated, under seal, as part of the record.

(d) Recess to Examine a Statement. The court may recess the proceedings to allow time for a party to examine the statement and prepare for its use.

(e) Sanction for Failure to Produce or Deliver a Statement. If the party who called the witness disobeys an order to produce or deliver a statement, the court must strike the witness's testimony from the record. If an attorney for the government disobeys the order, the court must declare a mistrial if justice so requires.

(f) "Statement" Defined. As used in this rule, a witness's "statement" means:

(1) a written statement that the witness makes and signs, or otherwise adopts or approves;

(2) a substantially verbatim, contemporaneously recorded recital of the witness's oral statement that is contained in any recording or any transcription of a recording; or

(3) the witness's statement to a grand jury, however taken or recorded, or a transcription of such a statement.

(g) Scope. This rule applies at trial, at a suppression hearing under Rule 12, and to the extent specified in the following rules:

(1) Rule 5.1(h) (preliminary hearing);

(2) Rule 32(i)(2) (sentencing);

(3) Rule 32.1(e) (hearing to revoke or modify probation or supervised release);

(4) Rule 46(j) (detention hearing); and

(5) Rule 8 of the Rules Governing Proceedings under 28 U.S.C. § 2255.

Rule 26.3.

MISTRIAL

Before ordering a mistrial, the court must give each defendant and the government an opportunity to comment on the propriety of the order, to state whether that party consents or objects, and to suggest alternatives.

Rule 29.

MOTION FOR A JUDGMENT OF ACQUITTAL

(a) Before Submission to the Jury. After the government closes its evidence or after the close of all the evidence, the court on the defendant's motion must enter a judgment of acquittal of any offense for which the evidence is insufficient to sustain a conviction. The court may on its own consider whether the evidence is insufficient to sustain a conviction. If the court denies a motion for a judgment of acquittal at the close of the government's evidence, the defendant may offer evidence without having reserved the right to do so.

(b) Reserving Decision. The court may reserve decision on the motion, proceed with the trial (where the motion is made before the close of all the evidence), submit the case to the jury, and decide the motion either before the jury returns a verdict or after it returns a verdict of guilty or is discharged without having returned a verdict. If the court reserves decision, it must decide the motion on the basis of the evidence at the time the ruling was reserved.

(c) After Jury Verdict or Discharge.

(1) ***Time for a Motion.*** A defendant may move for a judgment of acquittal, or renew such a motion, within 7 days after a guilty verdict or after the court discharges the jury, whichever is later, or within any other time the court sets during the 7-day period.

(2) ***Ruling on the Motion.*** If the jury has returned a guilty verdict, the court may set aside the verdict and enter an acquittal. If the jury has failed to return a verdict, the court may enter a judgment of acquittal.

(3) ***No Prior Motion Required.*** A defendant is not required to move for a judgment of acquittal before the court submits the case to the jury as a prerequisite for making such a motion after jury discharge.

(d) Conditional Ruling on a Motion for a New Trial.

(1) ***Motion for a New Trial.*** If the court enters a judgment of acquittal after a guilty verdict, the court must also conditionally determine whether any motion for a new trial should be granted if the judgment of acquittal is later vacated or reversed. The court must specify the reasons for that determination.

(2) ***Finality.*** The court's order conditionally granting a motion for a new trial does not affect the finality of the judgment of acquittal.

(3) ***Appeal.***

(A) *Grant of a Motion for a New Trial.* If the court conditionally grants a motion for a new trial and an appellate court later reverses the judgment of acquittal, the trial court must proceed with the new trial unless the appellate court orders otherwise.

(B) *Denial of a Motion for a New Trial.* If the court conditionally denies a motion for a new trial, an appellee may assert that the denial was erroneous. If the appellate court later reverses the judgment of acquittal, the trial court must proceed as the appellate court directs.

Rule 29.1.

CLOSING ARGUMENT

Closing arguments proceed in the following order:

(a) the government argues;

(b) the defense argues; and

(c) the government rebuts.

Rule 30.

JURY INSTRUCTIONS

(a) In General. Any party may request in writing that the court instruct the jury on the law as specified in the request. The request must be made at the close of the evidence or at any earlier time that the court reasonably sets. When the request is made, the requesting party must furnish a copy to every other party.

(b) Ruling on a Request. The court must inform the parties before closing argument show it intends to rule on the requested instructions.

(c) Time for Giving Instructions. The court may instruct the jury before or after the arguments are completed, or at both times.

(d) Objections to Instructions. A party who objects to any portion of the instructions or to a failure to give a requested instruction must inform the court of the specific objection and the grounds for the objection before the jury retires to deliberate. An opportunity must be given to object out of the jury's hearing and, on request, out of the jury's presence. Failure to object in accordance with this rule precludes appellate review, except as permitted under Rule 52(b).

Rule 31.

JURY VERDICT

(a) Return. The jury must return its verdict to a judge in open court. The verdict must be unanimous.

(b) Partial Verdicts, Mistrial, and Retrial.

(1) ***Multiple Defendants.*** If there are multiple defendants, the jury may return a verdict at any time during its deliberations as to any defendant about whom it has agreed.

(2) ***Multiple Counts.*** If the jury cannot agree on all counts as to any defendant, the jury may return a verdict on those counts on which it has agreed.

(3) ***Mistrial and Retrial.*** If the jury cannot agree on a verdict on one or more counts, the court may declare a mistrial on those counts. The government may retry any defendant on any count on which the jury could not agree.

(c) Lesser Offense or Attempt. A defendant may be found guilty of any of the following:

(1) an offense necessarily included in the offense charged;

(2) an attempt to commit the offense charged; or

(3) an attempt to commit an offense necessarily included in the offense charged, if the attempt is an offense in its own right.

(d) Jury Poll. After a verdict is returned but before the jury is discharged, the court must on a party's request, or may on its own, poll the jurors individually. If the poll reveals a lack of unanimity, the court may direct the jury to deliberate further or may declare a mistrial and discharge the jury.

Rule 32.

SENTENCING AND JUDGMENT

(a) Definitions. The following definitions apply under this rule:

(1) "Crime of violence or sexual abuse" means:

(A) a crime that involves the use, attempted use, or threatened use of physical force against another's person or property; or

(B) a crime under 18 U.S.C. §§ 2241–2248 or §§ 2251–2257.

(2) "Victim" means an individual against whom the defendant committed an offense for which the court will impose sentence.

(b) Time of Sentencing.

(1) *In General.* The court must impose sentence without unnecessary delay.

(2) *Changing Time Limits.* The court may, for good cause, change any time limits prescribed in this rule.

(c) Presentence Investigation.

(1) *Required Investigation.*

(A) *In General.* The probation officer must conduct a presentence investigation and submit a report to the court before it imposes sentence unless:

(i) 18 U.S.C. § 3593(c) or another statute requires otherwise; or

(ii) the court finds that the information in the record enables it to meaningfully exercise its sentencing authority under 18 U.S.C. § 3553, and the court explains its finding on the record.

(B) *Restitution.* If the law requires restitution, the probation officer must conduct an investigation and submit a report that contains sufficient information for the court to order restitution.

(2) *Interviewing the Defendant.* The probation officer who interviews a defendant as part of a presentence investigation must, on request, give the defendant's attorney notice and a reasonable opportunity to attend the interview.

(d) Presentence Report.

(1) *Applying the Sentencing Guidelines.* The presentence report must:

(A) identify all applicable guidelines and policy statements of the Sentencing Commission;

(B) calculate the defendant's offense level and criminal history category;

(C) state the resulting sentencing range and kinds of sentences available;

(D) identify any factor relevant to:

(i) the appropriate kind of sentence, or

(ii) the appropriate sentence within the applicable sentencing range; and

(E) identify any basis for departing from the applicable sentencing range.

(2) *Additional Information.* The presentence report must also contain the following information:

(A) the defendant's history and characteristics, including:

(i) any prior criminal record;

(ii) the defendant's financial condition; and

(iii) any circumstances affecting the defendant's behavior that may be helpful in imposing sentence or in correctional treatment;

(B) verified information, stated in a nonargumentative style, that assesses the financial, social, psychological, and medical impact on any individual against whom the offense has been committed;

(C) when appropriate, the nature and extent of nonprison programs and resources available to the defendant;

(D) when the law provides for restitution, information sufficient for a restitution order;

(E) if the court orders a study under 18 U.S.C. § 3552(b), any resulting report and recommendation; and

(F) any other information that the court requires.

(3) ***Exclusions.*** The presentence report must exclude the following:

(A) any diagnoses that, if disclosed, might seriously disrupt a rehabilitation program;

(B) any sources of information obtained upon a promise of confidentiality; and

(C) any other information that, if disclosed, might result in physical or other harm to the defendant or others.

(e) Disclosing the Report and Recommendation.

(1) ***Time to Disclose.*** Unless the defendant has consented in writing, the probation officer must not submit a presentence report to the court or disclose its contents to anyone until the defendant has pleaded guilty or nolo contendere, or has been found guilty.

(2) ***Minimum Required Notice.*** The probation officer must give the presentence report to the defendant, the defendant's attorney, and an attorney for the government at least 35 days before sentencing unless the defendant waives this minimum period.

(3) ***Sentence Recommendation.*** By local rule or by order in a case, the court may direct the probation officer not to disclose to anyone other than the court the officer's recommendation on the sentence.

(f) Objecting to the Report.

(1) ***Time to Object.*** Within 14 days after receiving the presentence report, the parties must state in writing any objections, including objections to material information, sentencing guideline ranges, and policy statements contained in or omitted from the report.

(2) ***Serving Objections.*** An objecting party must provide a copy of its objections to the opposing party and to the probation officer.

(3) ***Action on Objections.*** After receiving objections, the probation officer may meet with the parties to discuss the objections. The probation officer may then investigate further and revise the presentence report as appropriate.

(g) Submitting the Report. At least 7 days before sentencing, the probation officer must submit to the court and to the parties the presentence report and an addendum containing any unresolved objections, the grounds for those objections, and the probation officer's comments on them.

(h) Notice of Possible Departure from Sentencing Guidelines. Before the court may depart from the applicable sentencing range on a ground not identified for departure either in the presentence report or in a party's prehearing submission, the court must give the parties reasonable notice that it is contemplating such a departure. The notice must specify any ground on which the court is contemplating a departure.

(i) Sentencing.

(1) ***In General.*** At sentencing, the court:

(A) must verify that the defendant and the defendant's attorney have read and discussed the presentence report and any addendum to the report;

(B) must give to the defendant and an attorney for the government a written summary of—or summarize in camera—any information excluded from the presentence report under Rule 32(d)(3) on which the court will rely in sentencing, and give them a reasonable opportunity to comment on that information;

(C) must allow the parties' attorneys to comment on the probation officer's determinations and other matters relating to an appropriate sentence; and

(D) may, for good cause, allow a party to make a new objection at any time before sentence is imposed.

(2) ***Introducing Evidence; Producing a Statement.*** The court may permit the parties to introduce evidence on the objections. If a witness testifies at sentencing, Rule 26.2(a)–(d) and (f) applies. If a party fails to comply with a Rule 26.2 order to produce a witness's statement, the court must not consider that witness's testimony.

(3) *Court Determinations.* At sentencing, the court:

(A) may accept any undisputed portion of the presentence report as a finding of fact;

(B) must—for any disputed portion of the presentence report or other controverted matter—rule on the dispute or determine that a ruling is unnecessary either because the matter will not affect sentencing, or because the court will not consider the matter in sentencing; and

(C) must append a copy of the court's determinations under this rule to any copy of the presentence report made available to the Bureau of Prisons.

(4) *Opportunity to Speak.*

(A) *By a Party.* Before imposing sentence, the court must:

(i) provide the defendant's attorney an opportunity to speak on the defendant's behalf;

(ii) address the defendant personally in order to permit the defendant to speak or present any information to mitigate the sentence; and

(iii) provide an attorney for the government an opportunity to speak equivalent to that of the defendant's attorney.

(B) *By a Victim.* Before imposing sentence, the court must address any victim of a crime of violence or sexual abuse who is present at sentencing and must permit the victim to speak or submit any information about the sentence. Whether or not the victim is present, a victim's right to address the court may be exercised by the following persons if present:

(i) a parent or legal guardian, if the victim is younger than 18 years or is incompetent; or

(ii) one or more family members or relatives the court designates, if the victim is deceased or incapacitated.

(C) *In Camera Proceedings.* Upon a party's motion and for good cause, the court may hear in camera any statement made under Rule 32(i)(4).

(j) Defendant's Right to Appeal.

(1) *Advice of a Right to Appeal.*

(A) *Appealing a Conviction.* If the defendant pleaded not guilty and was convicted, after sentencing the court must advise the defendant of the right to appeal the conviction.

(B) *Appealing a Sentence.* After sentencing—regardless of the defendant's plea—the court must advise the defendant of any right to appeal the sentence.

(C) *Appeal Costs.* The court must advise a defendant who is unable to pay appeal costs of the right to ask for permission to appeal in forma pauperis.

(2) *Clerk's Filing of Notice.* If the defendant so requests, the clerk must immediately prepare and file a notice of appeal on the defendant's behalf.

(k) Judgment.

(1) *In General.* In the judgment of conviction, the court must set forth the plea, the jury verdict or the court's findings, the adjudication, and the sentence. If the defendant is found not guilty or is otherwise entitled to be discharged, the court must so order. The judge must sign the judgment, and the clerk must enter it.

(2) *Criminal Forfeiture.* Forfeiture procedures are governed by Rule 32.2.

Rule 32.1.

REVOKING OR MODIFYING PROBATION OR SUPERVISED RELEASE

(a) Initial Appearance.

(1) *Person In Custody.* A person held in custody for violating probation or supervised release must be taken without unnecessary delay before a magistrate judge.

(A) If the person is held in custody in the district where an alleged violation occurred, the initial appearance must be in that district.

(B) If the person is held in custody in a district other than where an alleged violation occurred, the initial appearance must be in that district, or in an adjacent district if the appearance can occur more promptly there.

(2) *Upon a Summons.* When a person appears in response to a summons for violating probation or supervised release, a magistrate judge must proceed under this rule.

(3) *Advice.* The judge must inform the person of the following:

(A) the alleged violation of probation or supervised release;

(B) the person's right to retain counsel or to request that counsel be appointed if the person cannot obtain counsel; and

(C) the person's right, if held in custody, to a preliminary hearing under Rule 32.1(b)(1).

(4) *Appearance in the District With Jurisdiction.* If the person is arrested or appears in the district that has jurisdiction to conduct a revocation hearing—either originally or by transfer of jurisdiction—the court must proceed under Rule 32.1(b)–(e).

(5) *Appearance in a District Lacking Jurisdiction.* If the person is arrested or appears in a district that does not have jurisdiction to conduct a revocation hearing, the magistrate judge must:

(A) if the alleged violation occurred in the district of arrest, conduct a preliminary hearing under Rule 32.1(b) and either:

(i) transfer the person to the district that has jurisdiction, if the judge finds probable cause to believe that a violation occurred; or

(ii) dismiss the proceedings and so notify the court that has jurisdiction, if the judge finds no probable cause to believe that a violation occurred; or

(B) if the alleged violation did not occur in the district of arrest, transfer the person to the district that has jurisdiction if:

(i) the government produces certified copies of the judgment, warrant, and warrant application; and

(ii) the judge finds that the person is the same person named in the warrant.

(6) *Release or Detention.* The magistrate judge may release or detain the person under 18 U.S.C. § 3143(a) pending further proceedings. The burden of establishing that the person will not flee or pose a danger to any other person or to the community rests with the person.

(b) Revocation.

(1) *Preliminary Hearing.*

(A) *In General.* If a person is in custody for violating a condition of probation or supervised release, a magistrate judge must promptly conduct a hearing to determine whether there is probable cause to believe that a violation occurred. The person may waive the hearing.

(B) *Requirements.* The hearing must be recorded by a court reporter or by a suitable recording device. The judge must give the person:

(i) notice of the hearing and its purpose, the alleged violation, and the person's right to retain counsel or to request that counsel be appointed if the person cannot obtain counsel;

(ii) an opportunity to appear at the hearing and present evidence; and

(iii) upon request, an opportunity to question any adverse witness, unless the judge determines that the interest of justice does not require the witness to appear.

(C) *Referral.* If the judge finds probable cause, the judge must conduct a revocation hearing. If the judge does not find probable cause, the judge must dismiss the proceeding.

(2) *Revocation Hearing.* Unless waived by the person, the court must hold the revocation hearing within a reasonable time in the district having jurisdiction. The person is entitled to:

(A) written notice of the alleged violation;

(B) disclosure of the evidence against the person;

(C) an opportunity to appear, present evidence, and question any adverse witness unless the court determines that the interest of justice does not require the witness to appear; and

(D) notice of the person's right to retain counsel or to request that counsel be appointed if the person cannot obtain counsel.

(c) Modification.

(1) *In General.* Before modifying the conditions of probation or supervised release, the court must hold a hearing, at which the person has the right to counsel.

(2) *Exceptions.* A hearing is not required if:

(A) the person waives the hearing; or

(B) the relief sought is favorable to the person and does not extend the term of probation or of supervised release; and

(C) an attorney for the government has received notice of the relief sought, has had a reasonable opportunity to object, and has not done so.

(d) Disposition of the Case. The court's disposition of the case is governed by 18 U.S.C. § 3563 and § 3565 (probation) and § 3583 (supervised release).

(e) Producing a Statement. Rule 26.2(a)–(d) and (f) applies at a hearing under this rule. If a party fails to comply with a Rule 26.2 order to produce a witness's statement, the court must not consider that witness's testimony.

Rule 33.

NEW TRIAL

(a) Defendant's Motion. Upon the defendant's motion, the court may vacate any judgment and grant a new trial if the interest of justice so requires. If the case was tried without a jury, the court may take additional testimony and enter a new judgment.

(b) Time to File.

(1) ***Newly Discovered Evidence.*** Any motion for a new trial grounded on newly discovered evidence must be filed within 3 years after the verdict or finding of guilty. If an appeal is pending, the court may not grant a motion for a new trial until the appellate court remands the case.

(2) ***Other Grounds.*** Any motion for a new trial grounded on any reason other than newly discovered evidence must be filed within 7 days after the verdict or finding of guilty, or within such further time as the court sets during the 7-day period.

Rule 34.

ARRESTING JUDGMENT

(a) In General. Upon the defendant's motion or on its own, the court must arrest judgment if:

(1) the indictment or information does not charge an offense; or

(2) the court does not have jurisdiction of the charged offense.

(b) Time to File. The defendant must move to arrest judgment within 7 days after the court accepts a verdict or finding of guilty, or after a plea of guilty or nolo contendere, or within such further time as the court sets during the 7-day period.

Rule 35.

CORRECTING OR REDUCING A SENTENCE

(a) Correcting Clear Error. Within 7 days after sentencing, the court may correct a sentence that resulted from arithmetical, technical, or other clear error.

(b) Reducing a Sentence for Substantial Assistance.

(1) ***In General.*** Upon the government's motion made within one year of sentencing, the court may reduce a sentence if:

(A) the defendant, after sentencing, provided substantial assistance in investigating or prosecuting another person; and

(B) reducing the sentence accords with the Sentencing Commission's guidelines and policy statements.

(2) ***Later Motion.*** Upon the government's motion made more than one year after sentencing, the court may reduce a sentence if the defendant's substantial assistance involved:

(A) information not known to the defendant until one year or more after sentencing;

(B) information provided by the defendant to the government within one year of sentencing, but which did not become useful to the government until more than one year after sentencing; or

(C) information the usefulness of which could not reasonably have been anticipated by the defendant until more than one year after sentencing and which was promptly provided to the government after its usefulness was reasonably apparent to the defendant.

(3) *Evaluating Substantial Assistance.* In evaluating whether the defendant has provided substantial assistance, the court may consider the defendant's presentence assistance.

(4) *Below Statutory Minimum.* When acting under Rule 35(b), the court may reduce the sentence to a level below the minimum sentence established by statute.

Rule 38.

STAYING A SENTENCE OR A DISABILITY

(a) Death Sentence. The court must stay a death sentence if the defendant appeals the conviction or sentence.

(b) Imprisonment.

(1) *Stay Granted.* If the defendant is released pending appeal, the court must stay a sentence of imprisonment.

(2) *Stay Denied; Place of Confinement.* If the defendant is not released pending appeal, the court may recommend to the Attorney General that the defendant be confined near the place of the trial or appeal for a period reasonably necessary to permit the defendant to assist in preparing the appeal.

(c) Fine. If the defendant appeals, the district court, or the court of appeals under Federal Rule of Appellate Procedure 8, may stay a sentence to pay a fine or a fine and costs. The court may stay the sentence on any terms considered appropriate and may require the defendant to:

(1) deposit all or part of the fine and costs into the district court's registry pending appeal;

(2) post a bond to pay the fine and costs; or

(3) submit to an examination concerning the defendant's assets and, if appropriate, order the defendant to refrain from dissipating assets.

(d) Probation. If the defendant appeals, the court may stay a sentence of probation. The court must set the terms of any stay.

(e) Restitution and Notice to Victims.

(1) ***In General.*** If the defendant appeals, the district court, or the court of appeals under Federal Rule of Appellate Procedure 8, may stay—on any terms considered appropriate—any sentence providing for restitution under 18 U.S.C. § 3556 or notice under 18 U.S.C. § 3555.

(2) ***Ensuring Compliance.*** The court may issue any order reasonably necessary to ensure compliance with a restitution order or a notice order after disposition of an appeal, including:

(A) a restraining order;

(B) an injunction;

(C) an order requiring the defendant to deposit all or part of any monetary restitution into the district court's registry; or

(D) an order requiring the defendant to post a bond.

(f) Forfeiture. A stay of a forfeiture order is governed by Rule 32.2(d).

(g) Disability. If the defendant's conviction or sentence creates a civil or employment disability under federal law, the district court, or the court of appeals under Federal Rule of Appellate Procedure 8, may stay the disability pending appeal on any terms considered appropriate. The court may issue any order reasonably necessary to protect the interest represented by the disability pending appeal, including a restraining order or an injunction.

Rule 41.

SEARCH AND SEIZURE

(a) Scope and Definitions.

(1) ***Scope.*** This rule does not modify any statute regulating search or seizure, or the issuance and execution of a search warrant in special circumstances.

(2) ***Definitions.*** The following definitions apply under this rule:

(A) "Property" includes documents, books, papers, any other tangible objects, and information.

(B) "Daytime" means the hours between 6:00 a.m. and 10:00 p.m. according to local time.

(C) "Federal law enforcement officer" means a government agent (other than an attorney for the government) who is engaged in enforcing the criminal laws and is within any category of officers authorized by the Attorney General to request a search warrant.

(b) Authority to Issue a Warrant. At the request of a federal law enforcement officer or an attorney for the government:

(1) a magistrate judge with authority in the district—or if none is reasonably available, a judge of a state court of record in the district—has authority to issue a warrant to search for and seize a person or property located within the district;

(2) a magistrate judge with authority in the district has authority to issue a warrant for a person or property outside the district if the person or property is located within the district when the warrant is issued but might move or be moved outside the district before the warrant is executed; and

(3) a magistrate judge—in an investigation of domestic terrorism or international terrorism (as defined in 18 U.S.C. § 2331)—having authority in any district in which activities related to the terrorism may have occurred, may issue a warrant for a person or property within or outside that district.

(c) Persons or Property Subject to Search or Seizure. A warrant may be issued for any of the following:

(1) evidence of a crime;

(2) contraband, fruits of crime, or other items illegally possessed;

(3) property designed for use, intended for use, or used in committing a crime; or

(4) a person to be arrested or a person who is unlawfully restrained.

(d) Obtaining a Warrant.

(1) ***Probable Cause.*** After receiving an affidavit or other information, a magistrate judge or a judge of a state court of record must issue the warrant if there is probable cause to search for and seize a person or property under Rule 41(c).

(2) ***Requesting a Warrant in the Presence of a Judge.***

(A) *Warrant on an Affidavit.* When a federal law enforcement officer or an attorney for the government presents an affidavit in support of a warrant, the judge may require the affiant to appear personally and may examine under oath the affiant and any witness the affiant produces.

(B) *Warrant on Sworn Testimony.* The judge may wholly or partially dispense with a written affidavit and base a warrant on sworn testimony if doing so is reasonable under the circumstances.

(C) *Recording Testimony.* Testimony taken in support of a warrant must be recorded by a court reporter or by a suitable recording device, and the judge must file the transcript or recording with the clerk, along with any affidavit.

(3) *Requesting a Warrant by Telephonic or Other Means.*

(A) *In General.* A magistrate judge may issue a warrant based on information communicated by telephone or other appropriate means, including facsimile transmission.

(B) *Recording Testimony.* Upon learning that an applicant is requesting a warrant, a magistrate judge must:

(i) place under oath the applicant and any person on whose testimony the application is based; and

(ii) make a verbatim record of the conversation with a suitable recording device, if available, or by a court reporter, or in writing.

(C) *Certifying Testimony.* The magistrate judge must have any recording or court reporter's notes transcribed, certify the transcription's accuracy, and file a copy of the record and the transcription with the clerk. Any written verbatim record must be signed by the magistrate judge and filed with the clerk.

(D) *Suppression Limited.* Absent a finding of bad faith, evidence obtained from a warrant issued under Rule 41(d)(3)(A) is not subject to suppression on the ground that issuing the warrant in that manner was unreasonable under the circumstances.

(e) Issuing the Warrant.

(1) *In General.* The magistrate judge or a judge of a state court of record must issue the warrant to an officer authorized to execute it.

(2) *Contents of the Warrant.* The warrant must identify the person or property to be searched, identify any person or property to be seized, and designate the magistrate judge to whom it must be returned. The warrant must command the officer to:

(A) execute the warrant within a specified time no longer than 10 days;

(B) execute the warrant during the daytime, unless the judge for good cause expressly authorizes execution at another time; and

(C) return the warrant to the magistrate judge designated in the warrant.

(3) *Warrant by Telephonic or Other Means.* If a magistrate judge decides to proceed under Rule 41(d)(3)(A), the following additional procedures apply:

(A) *Preparing a Proposed Duplicate Original Warrant.* The applicant must prepare a "proposed duplicate original warrant" and must read or otherwise transmit the contents of that document verbatim to the magistrate judge.

(B) *Preparing an Original Warrant.* The magistrate judge must enter the contents of the proposed duplicate original warrant into an original warrant.

(C) *Modifications.* The magistrate judge may direct the applicant to modify the proposed duplicate original warrant. In that case, the judge must also modify the original warrant.

(D) *Signing the Original Warrant and the Duplicate Original Warrant.* Upon determining to issue the warrant, the magistrate judge must immediately sign the original warrant, enter on its face the exact time it is issued, and direct the applicant to sign the judge's name on the duplicate original warrant.

(f) Executing and Returning the Warrant.

(1) *Noting the Time.* The officer executing the warrant must enter on its face the exact date and time it is executed.

(2) *Inventory.* An officer present during the execution of the warrant must prepare and verify an inventory of any property seized. The officer must do so in the presence of another officer and the person from whom, or from whose premises, the property was taken. If either one is not present, the officer must prepare and verify the inventory in the presence of at least one other credible person.

(3) *Receipt.* The officer executing the warrant must:

(A) give a copy of the warrant and a receipt for the property taken to the person from whom, or from whose premises, the property was taken; or

(B) leave a copy of the warrant and receipt at the place where the officer took the property.

(4) *Return.* The officer executing the warrant must promptly return it—together with a copy of the inventory—to the magistrate judge designated on the warrant. The judge must, on request, give a copy of the inventory to the person from whom, or from whose premises, the property was taken and to the applicant for the warrant.

(g) Motion to Return Property. A person aggrieved by an unlawful search and seizure of property or by the deprivation of property may move for the property's return. The motion must be filed in the district where the property was seized. The court must receive evidence on any factual issue necessary to decide the motion. If it grants the motion, the court must return the property to the movant, but may impose reasonable conditions to protect access to the property and its use in later proceedings.

(h) Motion to Suppress. A defendant may move to suppress evidence in the court where the trial will occur, as Rule 12 provides.

(i) Forwarding Papers to the Clerk. The magistrate judge to whom the warrant is returned must attach to the warrant a copy of the return, of the inventory, and of all other related papers and must deliver them to the clerk in the district where the property was seized.

Rule 43.

DEFENDANT'S PRESENCE

(a) When Required. Unless this rule, Rule 5, or Rule 10 provides otherwise, the defendant must be present at:

(1) the initial appearance, the initial arraignment, and the plea;

(2) every trial stage, including jury impanelment and the return of the verdict; and

(3) sentencing.

(b) When Not Required. A defendant need not be present under any of the following circumstances:

(1) ***Organizational Defendant.*** The defendant is an organization represented by counsel who is present.

(2) ***Misdemeanor Offense.*** The offense is punishable by fine or by imprisonment for not more than one year, or both, and with the defendant's written consent, the court permits arraignment, plea, trial, and sentencing to occur in the defendant's absence.

(3) ***Conference or Hearing on a Legal Question.*** The proceeding involves only a conference or hearing on a question of law.

(4) ***Sentence Correction.*** The proceeding involves the correction or reduction of sentence under Rule 35 or 18 U.S.C. § 3582(c).

(c) Waiving Continued Presence.

(1) ***In General.*** A defendant who was initially present at trial, or who had pleaded guilty or nolo contendere, waives the right to be present under the following circumstances:

(A) when the defendant is voluntarily absent after the trial has begun, regardless of whether the court informed the defendant of an obligation to remain during trial;

(B) in a noncapital case, when the defendant is voluntarily absent during sentencing; or

(C) when the court warns the defendant that it will remove the defendant from the courtroom for disruptive behavior, but the defendant persists in conduct that justifies removal from the courtroom.

(2) ***Waiver's Effect.*** If the defendant waives the right to be present, the trial may proceed to completion, including the verdict's return and sentencing, during the defendant's absence.

Rule 44.

RIGHT TO AND APPOINTMENT OF COUNSEL

(a) Right to Appointed Counsel. A defendant who is unable to obtain counsel is entitled to have counsel appointed to represent the defendant at every stage of the proceeding from initial appearance through appeal, unless the defendant waives this right.

(b) Appointment Procedure. Federal law and local court rules govern the procedure for implementing the right to counsel.

(c) Inquiry Into Joint Representation.

(1) ***Joint Representation.*** Joint representation occurs when:

(A) two or more defendants have been charged jointly under Rule 8(b) or have been joined for trial under Rule 13; and

(B) the defendants are represented by the same counsel, or counsel who are associated in law practice.

(2) ***Court's Responsibilities in Cases of Joint Representation.*** The court must promptly inquire about the propriety of joint representation and must personally advise each defendant of the right to the effective assistance of counsel, including separate representation. Unless there is good cause to believe that no conflict of interest is likely to arise, the court must take appropriate measures to protect each defendant's right to counsel.

Rule 48.

DISMISSAL

(a) By the Government. The government may, with leave of court, dismiss an indictment, information, or complaint. The government may not dismiss the prosecution during trial without the defendant's consent.

(b) By the Court. The court may dismiss an indictment, information, or complaint if unnecessary delay occurs in:

(1) presenting a charge to a grand jury;

(2) filing an information against a defendant; or

(3) bringing a defendant to trial.

Rule 52.

HARMLESS AND PLAIN ERROR

(a) Harmless Error. Any error, defect, irregularity, or variance that does not affect substantial rights must be disregarded.

(b) Plain Error. A plain error that affects substantial rights may be considered even though it was not brought to the court's attention.

Rule 58.

PETTY OFFENSES AND OTHER MISDEMEANORS

(a) Scope.

(1) ***In General.*** These rules apply in petty offense and other misdemeanor cases and on appeal to a district judge in a case tried by a magistrate judge, unless this rule provides otherwise.

(2) ***Petty Offense Case Without Imprisonment.*** In a case involving a petty offense for which no sentence of imprisonment will be imposed, the court may follow any provision of these rules that is not inconsistent with this rule and that the court considers appropriate.

(3) ***Definition.*** As used in this rule, the term "petty offense for which no sentence of imprisonment will be imposed" means a petty offense for which the court determines that, in the event of conviction, no sentence of imprisonment will be imposed.

(b) Pretrial Procedure.

(1) ***Charging Document.*** The trial of a misdemeanor may proceed on an indictment, information, or complaint. The trial of a petty offense may also proceed on a citation or violation notice.

(2) ***Initial Appearance.*** At the defendant's initial appearance on a petty offense or other misdemeanor charge, the magistrate judge must inform the defendant of the following:

(A) the charge, and the minimum and maximum penalties, including imprisonment, fines, any special assessment under 18 U.S.C. § 3013, and restitution under 18 U.S.C. § 3556;

(B) the right to retain counsel;

(C) the right to request the appointment of counsel if the defendant is unable to retain counsel—unless the charge is a petty offense for which the appointment of counsel is not required;

(D) the defendant's right not to make a statement, and that any statement made may be used against the defendant;

(E) the right to trial, judgment, and sentencing before a district judge—unless:

(i) the charge is a petty offense; or

(ii) the defendant consents to trial, judgment, and sentencing before a magistrate judge;

(F) the right to a jury trial before either a magistrate judge or a district judge—unless the charge is a petty offense; and

(G) if the defendant is held in custody and charged with a misdemeanor other than a petty offense, the right to a preliminary hearing under Rule 5.1, and the general circumstances, if any, under which the defendant may secure pretrial release.

(3) *Arraignment.*

(A) *Plea Before a Magistrate Judge.* A magistrate judge may take the defendant's plea in a petty offense case. In every other misdemeanor case, a magistrate judge may take the plea only if the defendant consents either in writing or on the record to be tried before a magistrate judge and specifically waives trial before a district judge. The defendant may plead not guilty, guilty, or (with the consent of the magistrate judge) nolo contendere.

(B) *Failure to Consent.* Except in a petty offense case, the magistrate judge must order a defendant who does not consent to trial before a magistrate judge to appear before a district judge for further proceedings.

(c) Additional Procedures in Certain Petty Offense Cases. The following procedures also apply in a case involving a petty offense for which no sentence of imprisonment will be imposed:

(1) *Guilty or Nolo Contendere Plea.* The court must not accept a guilty or nolo contendere plea unless satisfied that the defendant understands the nature of the charge and the maximum possible penalty.

(2) *Waiving Venue.*

(A) *Conditions of Waiving Venue.* If a defendant is arrested, held, or present in a district different from the one where the indictment, information, complaint, citation, or violation notice is pending, the defendant may state in writing a desire to plead guilty or nolo contendere; to waive venue and trial in the district where the proceeding is pending; and to consent to the court's disposing of the case in the district where the defendant was arrested, is held, or is present.

(B) *Effect of Waiving Venue.* Unless the defendant later pleads not guilty, the prosecution will proceed in the district where the defendant was arrested, is held, or is present. The district clerk must notify the clerk in the original district of the defendant's waiver of venue. The defendant's statement of a desire to plead guilty or nolo contendere is not admissible against the defendant.

(3) *Sentencing.* The court must give the defendant an opportunity to be heard in mitigation and then proceed immediately to sentencing. The court may, however, postpone sentencing to allow the probation service to investigate or to permit either party to submit additional information.

(4) ***Notice of a Right to Appeal.*** After imposing sentence in a case tried on a not-guilty plea, the court must advise the defendant of a right to appeal the conviction and of any right to appeal the sentence. If the defendant was convicted on a plea of guilty or nolo contendere, the court must advise the defendant of any right to appeal the sentence.

(d) Paying a Fixed Sum in Lieu of Appearance.

(1) ***In General.*** If the court has a local rule governing forfeiture of collateral, the court may accept a fixed-sum payment in lieu of the defendant's appearance and end the case, but the fixed sum may not exceed the maximum fine allowed by law.

(2) ***Notice to Appear.*** If the defendant fails to pay a fixed sum, request a hearing, or appear in response to a citation or violation notice, the district clerk or a magistrate judge may issue a notice for the defendant to appear before the court on a date certain. The notice may give the defendant an additional opportunity to pay a fixed sum in lieu of appearance. The district clerk must serve the notice on the defendant by mailing a copy to the defendant's last known address.

(3) ***Summons or Warrant.*** Upon an indictment, or upon a showing by one of the other charging documents specified in Rule 58(b)(1) of probable cause to believe that an offense has been committed and that the defendant has committed it, the court may issue an arrest warrant or, if no warrant is requested by an attorney for the government, a summons. The showing of probable cause must be made under oath or under penalty of perjury, but the affiant need not appear before the court. If the defendant fails to appear before the court in response to a summons, the court may summarily issue a warrant for the defendant's arrest.

(e) Recording the Proceedings. The court must record any proceedings under this rule by using a court reporter or a suitable recording device.

(f) New Trial. Rule 33 applies to a motion for a new trial.

(g) Appeal.

(1) ***From a District Judge's Order or Judgment.*** The Federal Rules of Appellate Procedure govern an appeal from a district judge's order or a judgment of conviction or sentence.

(2) ***From a Magistrate Judge's Order or Judgment.***

(A) *Interlocutory Appeal.* Either party may appeal an order of a magistrate judge to a district judge within 10 days of its entry if a district judge's order could similarly be appealed. The party appealing must file a notice with the clerk specifying the order being appealed and must serve a copy on the adverse party.

(B) *Appeal from a Conviction or Sentence.* A defendant may appeal a magistrate judge's judgment of conviction or sentence to a district judge within 10 days of its entry. To appeal, the defendant must file a notice with the clerk specifying the judgment being appealed and must serve a copy on an attorney for the government.

(C) *Record.* The record consists of the original papers and exhibits in the case; any transcript, tape, or other recording of the proceedings; and a certified copy of the docket entries. For purposes of the appeal, a copy of the record of the proceedings must be made available to a defendant who establishes by affidavit an inability to pay or give security for the record. The Director of the Administrative Office of the United States Courts must pay for those copies.

(D) *Scope of Appeal.* The defendant is not entitled to a trial de novo by a district judge. The scope of the appeal is the same as in an appeal to the court of appeals from a judgment entered by a district judge.

(3) *Stay of Execution and Release Pending Appeal.* Rule 38 applies to a stay of a judgment of conviction or sentence. The court may release the defendant pending appeal under the law relating to release pending appeal from a district court to a court of appeals.

†